THE BEDFORD SERIES IN HISTORY AND CULTURE

Islam in the Indian Ocean World

A Brief History with Documents

THE BEDFORD SERIES IN HISTORY AND CULTURE

Islam in the Indian Ocean World
A Brief History with Documents

Omar H. Ali

University of North Carolina at Greensboro

Bedford/St. Martin's
A Macmillan Education Imprint

Boston • New York

For Bedford/St. Martin's

Vice President, Editorial, Macmillan Higher Education Humanities: Edwin Hill
Publisher for History: Michael Rosenberg
Senior Executive Editor for History: William J. Lombardo
Director of Development for History: Jane Knetzger
Developmental Editor: Kathryn Abbott
Editorial Assistant: Alexandra DeConti
Executive Marketing Manager: Sandra McGuire
Production Editor: Lidia MacDonald-Carr
Assistant Production Supervisor: Victoria Anzalone
Photo Editor: Robin Fadool
Text Permissions Manager: Kalina Ingham
Cover Design: William Boardman
Cover Art: Bibliotheque Nationale, Paris, France/DeAgostini Picture Library/
    Bridgeman Images.
Author Photo: Martin W. Kane/UNCG University Relations
Project Management: Books By Design, Inc.
Cartographer: Mapping Specialists, Ltd.
Composition: Achorn International, Inc.
Printing and Binding: RR Donnelley and Sons

Manufactured in the United States of America.

0   9   8   7   6   5
f   e   d   c   b   a

For information, write: Bedford/St. Martin's, 75 Arlington Street, Boston, MA 02116
    (617-399-4000)

ISBN 978-1-4576-0977-0

Acknowledgments

Text acknowledgments and copyrights appear at the back of the book on page 147, which constitutes an extension of the copyright page. Art acknowledgments and copyrights appear on the same page as the art selections they cover. It is a violation of the law to reproduce these selections by any means whatsoever without the written permission of the copyright holder.

At the time of publication all Internet URLs published in this text were found to accurately link to their intended Web site. If you do find a broken link, please forward the information to history@macmillan.com so that it can be corrected for the next printing.

Foreword

The Bedford Series in History and Culture is designed so that readers can study the past as historians do.

The historian's first task is finding the evidence. Documents, letters, memoirs, interviews, pictures, movies, novels, or poems can provide facts and clues. Then the historian questions and compares the sources. There is more to do than in a courtroom, for hearsay evidence is welcome, and the historian is usually looking for answers beyond act and motive. Different views of an event may be as important as a single verdict. How a story is told may yield as much information as what it says.

Along the way the historian seeks help from other historians and perhaps from specialists in other disciplines. Finally, it is time to write, to decide on an interpretation and how to arrange the evidence for readers.

Each book in this series contains an important historical document or group of documents, each document a witness from the past and open to interpretation in different ways. The documents are combined with some element of historical narrative — an introduction or a biographical essay, for example — that provides students with an analysis of the primary source material and important background information about the world in which it was produced.

Each book in the series focuses on a specific topic within a specific historical period. Each provides a basis for lively thought and discussion about several aspects of the topic and the historian's role. Each is short enough (and inexpensive enough) to be a reasonable one-week assignment in a college course. Whether as classroom or personal reading, each book in the series provides firsthand experience of the challenge — and fun — of discovering, recreating, and interpreting the past.

Lynn Hunt
David W. Blight
Bonnie G. Smith

To my colleagues *Alyssa Gabbay* and *Asa Eger*
of the Islamic Studies Research Network, and Ayah Khalifa,
Faris Almubaslat, Duaa Altholaya, Yasmin Ali, Abdelrahman
Elnoush, and Lena Ragab of the Muslim Student Association
at the University of North Carolina at Greensboro

لا إكراه في الدين

Let there be no compulsion in religion.

Qur'an 2:256

Preface

This book is a response to growing attention to and interest in premodern forms of globalization and efforts to better understand Islam in a larger geographical and historical context. It includes documents from the early modern era related to East Africa, the Middle East, South Asia, and, to a lesser extent, Southeast Asia in order to illustrate the critical role that Islam played in shaping the Indian Ocean world. Understanding this role and the ways in which Islam itself was transformed as it spread across the region largely through Muslim merchants is vital to understanding globalization in this era. The introduction and the documents that follow provide a sweeping look at an extended moment in world history that will help students gain a greater appreciation of the importance of Islam in facilitating globalization.

Part one details the ways in which Islam itself was transformed as it spread across the Indian Ocean world and how this vast region was transformed with the introduction of Islam—what is here called the Afro-Asianization of Islam and the Islamization of the Indian Ocean world. Islam as a religion, a set of practices, and a culture took on the characteristics of the people and societies to which it spread. Meanwhile, these people and societies changed in response to the introduction and deepening influence of Islam. After briefly describing the formation of Islam in western Arabia and its spread across the Middle East, East Africa, India, and Southeast Asia, the introduction pays particular attention to the ways in which the religion took shape beyond the Arabian Peninsula. It puts this expansion in context, explaining how Muslim merchants used trade to spread their religion and culture. The result was a dynamic interaction as local leaders adopted the faith and supported Islamic intellectual, artistic, and cultural developments even as they helped facilitate trade.

The documents in part two provide the evidentiary basis for understanding the interaction of Islam and trade in the Indian Ocean world. These documents (including memoirs, letters, travelogues, manuscripts, poems, royal decrees, sacred and legal texts, and transcriptions of oral stories), which date from the twelfth to the seventeenth centuries, attest to the complex and dynamic world created by Muslim traders. Written by merchants, navigators, court officials, ambassadors, Sufis, sultans, philosophers, administrators, theologians, poets, explorers, and legal scholars, the selections are organized into six chapters covering specific travelers (Ibn Battuta, Marco Polo, and Zheng He); trade, society, and social customs; Islamic law and teachings; Muslim polities and politics; conversion and religious practice; and pluralism, syncretism, and reaction. They were originally written in a broad range of languages, including Arabic, Persian, Gujarati, Urdu, Mandarin, Malay, and several European languages. To facilitate student analysis, a headnote provides the context for each document.

Following the documents are a chronology, questions for consideration, and a selected bibliography of key secondary sources. A map of the Indian Ocean world in the introduction helps orient students to the cities and societies, discussed throughout, that are particularly important in understanding trade networks and centers for the transmission of a range of products, people, and practices. Finally, numerous gloss notes define unfamiliar or difficult terms. Taken as a whole, this book is a tool for understanding Islam in world history.

ACKNOWLEDGMENTS

I am grateful to Bonnie Smith, the ever insightful and supportive Bedford Series in History and Culture advisory editor, for inviting me to put together this book. Among the many other people I would like to thank at Bedford/St. Martin's are Kathryn Abbott, Michael Rosenberg, Jane Knetzger, Arrin Kaplan, Alexandra DeConti, Traci Crowell, Laura Kintz, Lidia MacDonald-Carr, and Nancy Benjamin. I would also like to thank the following scholars for reviewing an early draft of the manuscript: Douglas Chambers, University of Southern Mississippi; Lucien Frary, Rider University; Chau Johnsen Kelly, University of North Florida; Malissa Taylor, University of Louisville; and Katya Vladimirov, Kennesaw State University. Bruce Holland and Yasmeen Chism were very helpful, as were Akbar Ahmed, Ned Alpers, Maggie Favretti, and Michelle Foreman, master teachers who inspire me. My colleagues Asa Eger and Alyssa Gabbay deserve special mention for their comradery and ongoing efforts to create spaces for people to learn about Islam in world history.

Finally, I am most grateful to my darling *bivi* for her loving and steadfast support; our little ones, Samina and Pablo; and my dearest Abu for his always wonderful comments, enthusiasm, and uplifting words.

Omar H. Ali

Contents

THE BEDFORD SERIES IN HISTORY AND CULTURE

Islam in the
Indian Ocean World

A Brief History with Documents

PART ONE

Introduction: Expansion and Transformation of Islam in the Indian Ocean World

MUHAMMAD AND THE *UMMAH*

Islam, the religion or cultural identity of more than 1.6 billion people in the world, began as a small community of monotheists in western Arabia during the early seventh century. Their leader, Muhammad Ibn Abdullah (the Prophet), a merchant turned mystic from Mecca, offered a simple yet compelling message: *There is only one god, Allah, and no other.*

Under the control of the polytheistic tribal rulers called the Quraish, Mecca was a crossroads of people, products, and ideas. If and when religious disputes arose, the Quraish tended to stay above the fray, as various preachers, pilgrims, and peddlers regularly passed through the bustling town. But when Muhammad began to publicly denounce the Quraish for their polytheism (in addition to challenging those who he believed had corrupted the original religion of Abraham by introducing concepts that moved away from the notion of a single, undivided god), he crossed the line.

Persecuted, Muhammad and his followers fled Mecca in 622, to the town of Yathrib, soon to be called Medina, a flight that would later become known as the Hijra and would mark the first year of the Muslim calendar. While greatly outnumbered by the Quraish, the Muslims were bolstered by several victories in the field. Over time, tribes from across the Arabian Peninsula joined the Muslim forces, and by 630 the

Muslims had organized themselves into an army that surged ten thousand strong. Not only would they seize the town of Mecca, but soon, like the powerful sandstorms that shifted the landscape out of which they came, they swept over the entire peninsula and took control of large parts of North Africa and West Asia. The *ummah*—the Muslim community—not only survived but thrived, growing in new directions, and in new ways.

ISLAMIZATION AND AFRO-ASIANIZATION

While Islam spread as a political force during its early years, trade largely drove its religious expansion thereafter. Muslim merchants played the decisive role in the adoption of Islam by non-Muslims. Prompted by the presence, example, and teachings of Muslims, people beyond Arabia integrated Islam into their own traditions. Over the following centuries, Muslims spread their faith, culture, and influence across the Indian Ocean world—the vast region encompassing East Africa, the Arabian Peninsula, southern Iraq and Iran, Pakistan, India, Sri Lanka, Malaysia, and the Indonesian archipelago (see map). Wherever Muslim merchants ventured, followed by Sufis (mystics) and scholars, new adherents made Islam their own, simultaneously expanding the *ummah* while reflecting the religion through their own cultures.

By the twelfth century, Islam had become a discernible part of societies across much of this region. As growing numbers of people identified themselves as Muslim, incorporating their perspectives and practices into the religion, not only did the Indian Ocean world become increasingly Islamized, but Islam—in its content, character, and composition—became both increasingly Africanized and Asianized. That is, it became Afro-Asianized.[1] East Africans practiced their own form of spiritualism alongside Muslim prayer rituals; meanwhile, Muslim rulers in South Asia allowed class distinctions to continue along the lines of the Hindu caste system. In these and other ways, Islam varied among Muslims across the region.

Over the course of several centuries, Islam would assume a wide range of forms by encompassing a great variety of people. The process was already evident in the earliest days and formation of the *ummah*, beginning with the figure of Bilal Ibn Rabah, who is among the first Muslims mentioned in Islamic sources. Born into slavery in Mecca to an Abyssinian mother and an Arab father, Bilal al-Habashi (the Ethiopian) heard Muhammad's message firsthand.[2] The Prophet, who had been

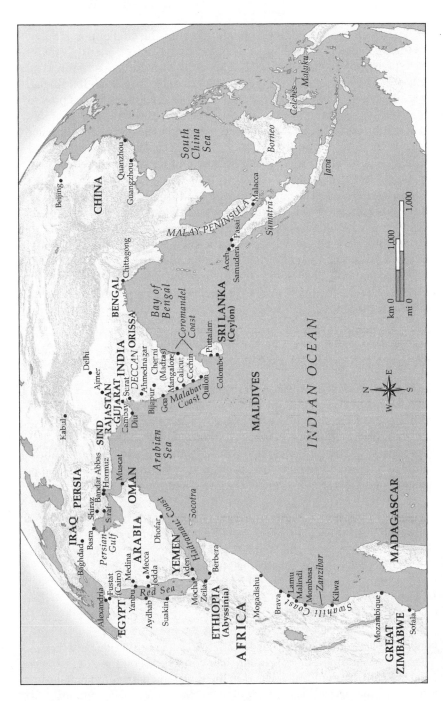

The Indian Ocean World, ca. 1450

3

orphaned as a child and knew something about the challenges of being an outsider, spoke of building an inclusive community under the single, merciful, compassionate god Allah. Moved by Muhammad's words, Bilal became a Muslim. Openly defying his slave master, Umayyah Ibn Khalaf, a member of the Quraish tribe who insisted that all of his slaves pray to the lower deities Lat and Uzza, Bilal professed his newfound faith. For this act of insubordination, he was tortured—forced to lie on the searing sand with a boulder placed on top of him. But even as Bilal was being crushed by the boulder and the additional weight of another slave ordered to sit on top, he refused to recant.

Hearing of the defiant Ethiopian, one of Muhammad's close companions, Abu Bakr, approached Umayyah to purchase Bilal, who went on to become a trusted companion of the Prophet and, most famously, Islam's first *mu'azzin*, the person who makes the call to prayer. Over the following years, decades, and centuries, Bilal's *Azzan*—the powerful, melodic call to prayer that begins with the declaration *Allah-u-akbar* (Allah is great)—would echo across the ever-expanding, ever-changing Muslim world (Document 12).

ARABIA AND MUSLIMS BEYOND THE PENINSULA

From the beginning, Muslims were diverse, not only in terms of their race and ethnicity but also in terms of their social and religious backgrounds. In a number of ways, Islam is a continuation of the Judeo-Christian traditions. For Muslims, Muhammad is the last in a long line of prophets, including Isa (Jesus), Musa (Moses), and Ibrahim (Abraham). In addition to Judaism and Christianity, Islam drew on and incorporated elements of other religious beliefs and practices. For example, the word *Allah*, which is a contraction of *al-ilah* (the god), had long been used by Arabs who believed in an originating creator god.[3]

The Qur'an, the guiding text for Muslims, is understood to be the word of Allah. According to Islamic tradition, the words contained in the Qur'an were revealed to Muhammad through the archangel Jibrael (Gabriel) beginning in 610 and continuing over the next twenty-two years. In addition to the Qur'an, Muslims follow the Hadith (or Sunna)—the collected oral accounts of the early Muslim community and the life and sayings of Muhammad—in determining Islamic laws and social conventions.[4] How the Qur'an and Hadith are interpreted has varied considerably over time and place and has caused major theological and legal divisions among Muslims, as in the divisions between the majority Sunni and minority Shi'a—in addition to the even smaller minority of

Ibadi Muslims. Such divisions are compounded by further distinctions among the Shi'a (Twelver, Isma'ili, and Zaydi) and among the multiple Sunni schools of Islamic law (Hanafi, Maliki, Shafi'i, and Hanbali, among others). Within Islam, there are also dozens of Sufi "brotherhoods," or *tariqas*, pursuing more contemplative, mystical spiritualism centered on particular *pirs* (saints). Sufi orders, which appeared within a few centuries of the founding of Islam, would come to include the Qadiriyyah, Chishti, Naqshbandi, and Ba'Alawiyya, among others. Beyond these divisions and distinctions are many more differences in how Islam is actually practiced.

Over time, Muslim merchants carrying a range of products and Islamic practices made their way into sub-Saharan Africa. They traveled either south in caravans from northern Africa across the Sahara or east by boat from the Arabian Peninsula down the East African coast. Muslim merchants similarly made their way by land and sea throughout much of Asia. By the tenth century, Muslims had reached both West Africa and West-Central Africa, as well as the Central Asian steppes, soon making regular contact with distant China. (Muslims had reached China as early as the seventh century via the Silk Road.[5]) By the twelfth century, Muslims had become part of vibrant merchant communities stretching from southern Arabia down the east coast of Africa and across the Arabian Sea to the west coast of India, reaching parts of the Indonesian archipelago in Southeast Asia.

Up through the twelfth century, most of the maritime trade pursued by Muslims was restricted to the western half of the Indian Ocean, with the eastern Indian Ocean trade largely dominated by Hindu merchants. Starting in the thirteenth century, however, Muslims began to also control the eastern trade. This change, the result of both shifting political conditions in China and greater Muslim mercantile success, brought Muslim merchants and Islam into Southeast Asia.

With the migration of Muslims beyond the Arabian Peninsula, a mix of Arab, followed by Persian and Turkic, social customs, including dress, diet, language, and rituals, were incorporated into local cultural and religious practices across the Indian Ocean world. In turn, as Arab, Persian, and Turkic Muslims were exposed to new cultures in Africa and Asia, the growing *ummah* reflected those new cultures. That is, wherever Muslims either took political control or became a regular presence through trade, local populations interpreted Islam in accordance with their own beliefs and social conventions, blending Muslim orthopraxy—what was deemed to be "correct" religious practice and behavior—with their own practices. Nowhere would people fully replace their own religious or social systems with the coming of Islam. As a result, the daily activities of Muslims outside the Arab heartlands often co-existed alongside the rules and regulations of orthodox comportment decided by the mostly Arab-oriented and -trained *ulema*, the official interpreters and codifiers of Islam (Document 19).

While Muslims outside of Arabia became increasingly less tied to Arab Muslims over the centuries, Arabia, the Arabic language, and Arab social conventions continued to permeate much of Islamic practices across much of the Indian Ocean world. The Muslim ritual of facing Mecca multiple times a day to pray was a constant reminder of the importance of Islam's holiest city. Muslims also learned Qur'anic verses and Muslim expressions in Arabic—such as the frequently heard *inshah'Allah* (god willing). These verses and expressions filled the markets, mosques, and homes of Muslims from the Horn of Africa to Sumatra.

Muslim merchants and sailors were joined by pilgrims crisscrossing the region. Those who were able undertook the Hajj, a pilgrimage to Mecca that takes place at a prescribed time each year based on the lunar calendar, or the Umrah, a pilgrimage at any other time. For those who completed the journey to Mecca, as well as the communities they returned to, the pilgrimage reinforced their ties to the Hijaz, the area of western Arabia encompassing the cities of Mecca and Medina. A Muslim's association with the Arabian Peninsula, Arabic, and Arab customs was, therefore, continually reaffirmed and reinforced.

As central as Arabia, its people, and its language were to Muslims, the spread of Islam was a process of adoption, assimilation, and integration into local systems—the fusion of religious traditions sometimes characterized as syncretism—and not simply a matter of conversion, which might imply the obliteration of former belief systems and practices in favor of some ideal form of Islam. In this way, Muslim merchants, starting with Arabs but soon including Persians, Turks, Africans, and Indians, among others, facilitated Islam's expansion across the Middle East, East Africa, South Asia, and Southeast Asia. Aiding these merchants were Islam's legal structures and shared social conventions.

MERCHANTS, LAW, AND CUSTOM

Along the coasts and across the Indian Ocean—the expansive body of water known by Greek cartographers as the Erythraean Sea, by their Chinese counterparts as the "Western Ocean," and by Arabs, Africans, and Indians by various other names—maritime trade would unify otherwise geographically distant people.[6] The opportunities and rewards that came with trade—whether in African ivory, gold, or mangrove poles; Indian textiles, spices, or tea; Chinese silks, steel, or porcelain; or slaves of various origins (largely captives of war)—would lead Muslim merchants to travel regularly over long distances using the seasonal monsoon winds and sea currents to guide them. Traders traveled aboard *dhows*, the name used for any number of sailing vessels with triangular sails in the western Indian Ocean. Southeast Asians used outrigger canoes, generally grouped under the name *perahus*, and Chinese traders employed large ships known as *junks* (with as many as nine masts and six hundred crew members), which circulated around the eastern part of the ocean.

Over time, seasonal migration driven by the monsoons led to Muslim migration and the creation or transformation of new cosmopolitan coastal societies, including the Swahili of East Africa, the Mappila of western India, and the Aceh Darussalam of Indonesia.[7] Such societies formed parts of an interconnected transcontinental world in which Muslims became leading economic players. Muslims, however, were hardly alone on the seas or on land. They joined a variety of centuries-old trade routes carved out by Jews, Armenians, Christians, and others from the Middle East and East Africa, along with Hindus from South Asia and Buddhists from Southeast Asia.

Long before the coming of Islam, Arabs had been exchanging goods with Hindus, as had Ethiopians with Chinese traders. The archaeological record reveals pre-Islamic Indian-minted coins in Ethiopia, for instance, as well as Chinese porcelain at sites along the East African coast dating several centuries before Muslims began making regular contact with the Horn of Africa and down the Swahili coast. In addition to the prized and common products traded by merchants across the Indian Ocean world, Muslim merchants introduced practical legal standards into existing trade routes that made economic exchange even more efficient wherever they were adopted.

Shari'a—Islamic codes of conduct, or law, governing credit, weights and measures, interest rates, and prices in ports and caravan towns across the region—created shared ways of conducting business, including the widespread use of bills of exchange, otherwise known as cheques (checks) over long distances. The use of such conventions led to the greater flow and volume of trade, despite the ongoing insecurity of seafaring and long-distance travel. In addition to powerful storms, merchants, sailors, and pilgrims had to contend with East African, Arab, Persian, Indian, Indonesian, and, later, Portuguese pirates on the prowl.

Captains, shipowners, and business agents took measures to protect themselves and their cargo, including arming their vessels or having armed escorts. During the twelfth century, the Fatimid government in Cairo employed the *karim*, an escort system comprising three or four armed ships that guarded merchant fleets traveling back and forth to India, and during the fourteenth century, individual merchants employed Abyssinian soldiers on ships off the western coasts of India and Sri Lanka for protection against pirates. As one impressed observer put it, these Abyssinians were the "guarantors of safety on the Indian Ocean."[8] Most captains, however, simply prayed and took their chances. Some Sufi brotherhoods specialized in offering *baraka* (spiritual protection). Even if military escorts or spiritual forces did not guarantee safety on the high seas, such practices gave seafarers a greater sense of security.

The enforcement of Islamic commercial law provided additional security. Because Shari'a tended to favor Muslim traders and financiers both implicitly and often explicitly, some pragmatic non-Muslims assumed Islamic identities, even if in name only. Meanwhile, within Islamic commercial law, differences based on pre-Muslim practices were common. Pre-Islamic local systems continued to operate alongside Muslim ones.

By the twelfth century, the majority Sunni branch of Islam had four major schools of law (Shafi'i, Hanafi, Hanbali, and Maliki), each named after a noted legal scholar. Two of these, Shafi'i and Hanafi, were the most widely used systems in the Indian Ocean world. Shafi'i was employed along the East African coast (the Horn of Africa and the Swahili coast), Yemen's Hadramaut coast, and throughout much of Indonesia; Hanafi was used in parts of India; Hanbali was widespread in Arabia (except in the southern area, known as Arabia Felix); meanwhile, Maliki, which was employed throughout North Africa outside of northeastern Egypt, was used in the Sudan. While there were some disagreements among the various schools over interpretations of the Qur'an and Hadith, the basic laws and precepts of all four systems were more similar than they were different (Document 14).

Reflecting Muhammad's own experience as a merchant, the Qur'an includes several verses that strongly encourage, even boast about, trade and the role of merchants in society and the afterlife. Two examples are "The merchant enjoys the felicity both of this world and the next" and "He who makes money pleases Allah."[9] Both Qur'anic and Hadith notions of fair and honest business practices also were incorporated into Islamic commercial law. On fairness, the Qur'an notes, for example, "Give a full measure when you measure and weigh with balanced scales;

this is fair, and better in the end" (Sura al-Isra, 17:35). The Hadith praises honesty as a virtue to be emulated; as Muhammad is reported to have said, "The honest merchant will be with Prophets, *sidiqs* [the truthful ones], and martyrs."[10]

Overseeing both the spirit and the letter of the law were official Muslim market inspectors, or *muhtasib*, who were established in ports across the Indian Ocean world by Qur'anic mandate. The *muhtasib* were responsible for checking the accuracy of weights and measures, while also making sure Muslims were observing their prescribed prayers and fasts. Although the Qur'an forbids charging interest on loans, some Muslim jurists interpreted this to mean that a certain amount of interest was permissible and only usury, or an excessively high rate of interest, was prohibited.

Although fairness in business was encouraged and codified, Muslim jurists created a hierarchy that favored Muslims over others when it came to customs rates. While Muslims were to be charged 2.5 percent of the value of goods, *dhimmis* ("protected people") were to be charged 5 percent. (*Dhimmis* were people living in areas ruled by Muslims who were allowed to keep their own faith. They included Jews, Christians, Zoroastrians, and in India, Hindus and Buddhists.) The customs rate for Muslims was equal to one-tenth of the value of goods; this income was reserved for Allah, a concept rooted in the Judeo-Christian traditions.[11] As noted previously, Islamic commercial law included other customary practices that either predated Islam or were borrowed from other legal systems in use locally, such as Hindu commercial law. These pre- or non-Muslim standards were especially pertinent in regard to areas such as fishing, convoy (a group of ships traveling together), and salvage (the rescuing of a disabled or wrecked ship or its cargo), as well as credit arrangements and trading partnerships.

With long distances, the limitations of travel due to the monsoons, the unpredictability of prices, and ongoing variations in weights and coinage, it became important for merchants to have business agents stationed far and wide. The system of business partnerships pioneered by Jewish traders and then adopted by Muslims included having financiers partner with one or more traders who would travel with their goods. When a trader arrived home from a commercial voyage, he would return his partner's money and share whatever profits he had made. Many close and enduring partnerships were formed in this way, including that of the Jewish-Adeni *nakhuda* (shipowner) Mahruz ben Jacob and his Tana-based Indian Hindu partner Tinbu, whose "bonds" were said to be of "inseparable friendship and brotherhood."[12] Such partnerships also allowed Muslims to avoid the stigma attached to collecting interest on loans.

While competition between Muslim and non-Muslim merchants was perhaps to be expected, and although Islamic jurisprudence generally brought Muslim merchants together, Islamic traders were still fundamentally competitors. During the twelfth century, Isma'ili Shi'a merchants from Fatimid Egypt, who were increasingly in conflict with Christian powers in the Mediterranean, enlisted business agents in the port of Aden and throughout the Indian Ocean world to help them compete more effectively with Sunni and Twelver Shi'a merchants. Sometimes the competition between Muslim traders was so fierce that it degenerated into accusations of un-Islamic practices.

Although Islamic commercial law was not always able to prevent such conflicts from arising, shared rituals, behaviors, and languages among Muslim merchants often kept hostilities from escalating. Commonalities included the way in which Muslims greeted one another, communal prayers at mosques, familiarity with stories from the Hadith and verses from the Qur'an, knowledge and use of the Arabic (or Persian) language, shared dietary restrictions and fasting requirements, social conventions regarding family, and, for many, Sufi brotherhood affiliation. Such customs, practices, and knowledge created cultural bonds that were generally good for both business and the propagation of Islam.[13]

Whether of the Sunni, Shi'a, or Ibadi branch of Islam, Muslim merchants appeared to enjoy a somewhat higher status and greater respectability than non-Muslims across much of the region. Part of this was a result of their reputation as successful businessmen. Indeed, it was widely known that many non-Muslims assumed Arab or Persian names simply to be competitive. Such was the case with one of Malacca's rulers, Iskandar Syah (or Shah), whose subjects continued to practice a combination of pre-Islamic forms of spiritualism, Hinduism, and Buddhism.

Muslim merchants were often accompanied on their travels by Sufis, scholars, or jurists from Arabia or other centers of Muslim learning. Their blessings, teachings, or prestige were welcomed by emerging or established Muslim rulers and communities. Sometimes the merchants themselves were Sufis, scholars, or jurists. One of these, Ibn Battuta, the fourteenth-century Moroccan jurist, recounts how he was warmly welcomed and given audience with local Muslim authorities at various ports from the Horn of Africa to the Maldives (Document 1). While most Muslim merchants were neither scholars nor Sufis, many were missionaries with at least a rudimentary knowledge of the Qur'an or

Hadith. Whether or not they proselytized, in one way or another they ended up introducing some aspects of Islam to the non-Muslims they encountered. Muslim missionaries, whether formally trained or not, followed in their wake, with the primary purpose of religious dissemination. Among the most effective of these missionaries were Sufis, whose mysticism and flexibility lent themselves to popular adoption of Islam (Documents 30, 31, and 35).[14]

SUFIS, ULEMA, AND SOCIETY

While Muslim merchants were among the first to introduce Islam across much of the Indian Ocean world, Sufis, scholars, and *qadis* (judges trained in Shari'a) brought a deeper appreciation of its spiritual dimensions, religious practices, and legal aspects and were often welcomed into new communities where Muslims lived. Muslim scholars and qadis tended toward orthodox views and practices (orthopraxy). They were more rigid and less accommodating of other ways of being than Sufis, who tended to promote more unorthodox views and practices (with notions of orthodox and unorthodox conduct varying, and blurring, depending on time and place). Whether visiting or permanently settling in an area, Muslims conducted business, taught, adjudicated, married, and had families, becoming inextricably linked to the people and culture of their new home. In turn, each new generation of Muslims shaped the practice of Islam in that place.

Thus, people from all ranks of society—rich and poor, sultans and slaves, scholars and servants, merchants and jurists, farmers and artisans—determined what it meant to be Muslim through their daily activities. Because of differences in power tied to class, gender, age, and ethnicity, however, the meaning of Islam evolved in uneven ways. Like other socioreligious institutions, Islam—conceptually and in practice—was a function of power and authority. Those with the most power and institutionalized forms of authority ultimately exerted the greatest influence on how it was understood and expressed in a given society. Among those who held sway were wealthier Muslim families and visiting dignitaries. Wherever Islam was adopted, particular interpretations of it were variously enforced through punishment or reward, either blatantly or more subtly. In some places, the principal authority was the local ulema, in others Sufis or the local ruler, and in still others individual family members. Often authority was shared among all of these people. In this way, Islam was most often a matter of local authority and political power

(including power within a given household). Those who were able to en-
force what they deemed Islamic tended to determine what was indeed
Islamic—but not always and not without pushback.

In contrast with the ulema, Sufis tended to be much more inclusive
of other traditions. The origins of Sufism go back to the mysticism of
the Prophet Muhammad, who according to early Islamic sources medi-
tated on Mount Hira. The first Sufis appear in records from the eighth
century as individuals engaged in similar meditation. It was not until the
eleventh century, however, that Sufism was more systematically organized into brotherhoods, or orders, based on the teachings of a particular Sufi master or saint. The attraction of Sufis across the Indian Ocean
world lay in their heterodoxy. Their openness made them successful
disseminators of Islam among people who were looking for a more personal spiritual experience—in contrast to the impersonal and technical legalism that had come to dominate much of Islamic teaching out
of the major centers of Muslim scholarship (including Mecca, Medina,
Cairo, Damascus, and Baghdad). Whereas in some cities educated Sufis
and ulema worked together, as in parts of northern India, Sufism in
the countryside often took eclectic forms that the ulema strenuously
opposed.

Sufi brotherhoods were known for providing merchants, travelers,
and pilgrims with a place to rest both in ports and along inland caravan
routes. One of the more popular Sufi brotherhoods among merchants
was the Kazaruniyya, named after the eleventh-century saint Abu Ishaq
Ibrahim Ibn Shahriyar, from Kazarun in Central Asia. In addition to offering lodging, the order provided *baraka*, or spiritual protection, through
its deceased founder, in return for payment from travelers upon their
safe arrival at their destinations. The Kazaruniyya order was active in
ports from Cambay, on India's west coast, to Canton, in southern China.
(Muslims also had formed an even larger community in Quanzhou,
north of Canton, where some of the most eminent Muslim families
dominated trade.) Sufis' perceived (or sometimes explicit) heterodoxy
was an ongoing source of consternation for the ulema.

Whatever their particular brand of Islam, being Muslim had slowly
become a valuable social identification across the region. Muslims, in
comparison to non-Muslims, tended to receive more privileges and
achieve higher social status, from paying lower taxes to gaining entry
into influential social and business circles. Indeed, by the twelfth century, most spectacularly during the Abbasid caliphate, Muslim rulers
were known for patronizing scholars, artists, and scientists and, as a
result, synthesizing and promoting the development of the arts, archi-

tecture, poetry, geography, literature, history, and philosophy, as well as mathematics, medicine, botany, astronomy, and engineering. The Delhi sultanate, followed by the Mughals, in northern India and the Bahmani and other sultanates in central India's Deccan were among the major patrons of the era. In many parts of the Indian Ocean world, assuming a Muslim identity therefore opened up the possibility for multiple benefits—wealth, prestige, education, and access to innovations in a variety of technical, intellectual, and artistic fields—that is, besides the spiritual dimensions of Islam.

Islam's ethical vision of egalitarianism was in ongoing tension with existing hierarchical social structures. Beyond the early years of the Muslim community, gender and/or class distinctions were overriding obstacles for most women and the poor.[15] Servants and slaves remained a permanent underclass, although some were able to rise through the ranks of society, and a few even gained extraordinary power and authority. Most famous among these was Malik Ambar, an Abyssinian slave who became de facto ruler of the Ahmednagar sultanate in the Deccan during the early seventeenth century (Document 25).

In terms of gender, few women, even those of the upper class, commanded the kind of authority their male counterparts were permitted to exert. Women did, however, play prominent roles in shaping the early *ummah*. Islam's first convert was Khadija bint Khuwaylid, Muhammad's wife of more than twenty-five years, and the influential Aisha bint Abu Bakr, who married Muhammad following Khadija's death, was a major source of the Hadith. Despite these and dozens of other women who fought, taught, and helped govern alongside men, Muslim orthodoxy became male dominated. Even as early as the eighth century, patriarchal Arab and Persian social conventions excluding women from the ulema took hold as that class of men began to coalesce as an institution. Orthodox Islam tended to reflect and reinforce existing patriarchy. By contrast, many of the unorthodox views and practices of Sufism allowed women to express themselves and assume leadership roles in relation to both men and women. Some women, such as the eighth-century Persian Sufi mystic Rabi'a al-Adawiyya and the fourteenth-century Gujarati Sidi (African-descended) Sufi Mai Mishra, rose to public prominence as saints.

In the Indian Ocean world of the early modern era, slavery was not racialized. Rather, slaves were people of different backgrounds who had been captured in war. While there are no verses in the Qur'an or lines in the Hadith that explicitly call for the abolition of slavery, the sacred texts encourage more humane treatment of enslaved people and offer several avenues for liberation, as in Sura an-Nur (Qur'an 24:33), which encourages masters to manumit slaves "if they are good and trustworthy," and Sura al-Balad (Qur'an 90:13), where masters are urged "to free a slave" as a righteous act. Islam prohibited the enslavement of fellow Muslims, although this teaching was not always followed in practice. The hierarchical reality of most sedentary societies was that the majority of people were in some form of *unfree* labor system, which Islam did little to disrupt.

Although slavery was not based on race until the modern era, notions of different races existed across the Indian Ocean world. Africans, Arabs, Indians, and Chinese were broadly considered different races, despite the enormous ethnic differences within these groups. Africans had been part of Indian Ocean communities outside of Africa since at least the first century. In light of the Islamic prohibition against enslaving Muslims, increasing numbers of Africans were taken from non-Muslim areas in interior sections of the continent and sold in the slave markets of East Africa and southern Arabia. From there, they were dispersed across the region. In addition, many Africans had long traveled on their own as merchants, sailors, and mercenaries. This voluntary migration, or movement, complemented the military slave system that funneled hundreds of thousands of enslaved Africans into the Middle East and South Asia during the early modern era. Over time, increasing numbers of enslaved Africans were employed as domestic servants, concubines, pearl divers, agricultural laborers, body guards, palace guards, and soldiers. Gradually, they were assimilated into many societies across the Indian Ocean world, adopting Islam and marrying local women, whose children were born free.

Travel by sea remained the principal way in which Islam reached the outermost reaches of the Indian Ocean. The great ocean made no distinctions based on gender, class, age, ethnicity, race, or caste. All fared equally well or poorly when at sea. Muslim merchants, followed by scholars and pilgrims, were more aided than not in their travels by the monsoons that propelled their ships. For approximately four months out of the year, from November through February, winds blowing in a southwesterly direction from China and India, accompanied by surface-level currents, carried the ships in one direction. Then, from April through August, when the winds reversed course, they propelled the same ships in the other direction. Captains and merchants planned their journeys according to these natural forces, and pilgrims followed suit. Muslim migration and trade were, therefore, dependent on the ocean, and the natural harbors, islands, and reefs that permitted access to markets along the coasts and farther inland.

Inland Muslim political powers, notably the Delhi sultanate followed by the Mughals, would also draw from the complex maritime networks of the Indian Ocean. But just as Islam flowed out from the Arabian Peninsula, so, too, did Islam take in the multiplicity of people and cultures from the societies of the Indian Ocean world. It was a process that entailed both the expansion and the transformation of the *ummah* with each new generation of adherents. With East Africa being closest in proximity to the Hijaz, Ethiopia and the wider Horn of Africa were naturally the earliest points of contact for Muslims who ventured beyond Arabia.

EAST AFRICA: ABYSSINIA AND THE SWAHILI COAST

Islam entered East Africa when the Ethiopian highlands became a haven for a number of persecuted Muslims from the Arabian Peninsula. The first groups of people who sought safety were refugees directed to leave by the Prophet. Muhammad believed they would find refuge in the Christian Ethiopian kingdom of Aksum, which they did under Aksum's king, al-Najashi Ashama Ibn Abjar, who would soon adopt Islam as his own. At the same time, the African presence in the early Muslim community of Mecca that began with Bilal and other Africans in the Hijaz continued as Muslims traveled back and forth between Arabia and East Africa or permanently migrated to other parts of the continent. This process was part of the Africanization of Islam and the Islamization of Africa. For Africans, Islamization included more than the adoption of the new faith or a Muslim identity. It also included new ways of life among the Bantu- and Cushitic-speaking people who, together with Arabs and other foreigners, created the vibrant cosmopolitan culture of the Swahili coast. Changes included those in language, material culture, architecture, funeral customs, writing, political institutions, and gender relations.[16]

Prior to the founding of Islam, Arabs, such as the Azd tribe of Oman, had been trading down the East African coast. This pattern of trade continued as Arabs became Muslim. Mosques constructed of coral rag (a type of limestone) in the Lamu archipelago—at Unguja Ukuu on Zanzibar Island and at Ras Mkumbuu on Pemba Island—date to the mid-eighth century, and the one constructed at Shanga (Pate Island) continued to be maintained into the fifteenth century. Meanwhile, African gold, mangrove poles (used for the construction of houses), resins (used for incense), ivory, and slaves were regularly sought in markets stretching from the Hadramaut to the Persian Gulf and western India. From the

Horn of Africa down the Swahili coast, Muslim traders came and went with the winds, but many eventually settled down there. Although some Muslims settled in this part of East Africa prior to the twelfth century, not until the thirteenth century did Ibadi Muslims—who came to dominate much of the coastline—begin to make permanent homes in the places where their forefathers had long been engaged in trade. These Swahili traders of increasingly mixed African and Arab descent developed a new language, Kiswahili, combining the linguistic structure of Bantu with a number of Arabic loan words, especially those associated with Muslim religious practices, and to a lesser extent Persian. The written form of Kiswahili used Arabic script.

Like their counterparts elsewhere in the Indian Ocean, these Afro-Arab Swahili traders used the monsoons to their advantage. Making their way up to the Horn and then across the Hadramaut, most returned with the monsoon cycle. Many others, however, continued up the Persian Gulf or across the Arabian Sea to Gujarat, in India. At the height of their trade in the thirteenth and fourteenth centuries, some forty trading towns dotted the East African coastline, including Zanzibar (Unguja), Lamu, Pemba, Kilwa, Malindi, and Mogadishu. Each of these towns—many turned city-states, with sultans leading the local polities—were aided by the seasonal winds, which made the central East African coast a natural point of arrival and departure for Indian Ocean sailors and traders. Over time, advancements in maritime technology made travel easier and more profitable. By the end of the twelfth century, merchants along the entire East African coast were part of the larger Muslim trading networks producing extraordinary wealth, albeit mostly concentrated in the hands of local merchants and monarchs. Elegant mosques, including the fourteenth-century palace complex Husuni Kubwa, were opulently decorated—some with carpets from Isfahan and Gujarat, ceramic ware from China, and exquisitely designed platters from Persia.[17]

In addition to the early-seventh-century Muslim migrants who sought political and religious asylum in Ethiopia, there were dissident Muslims—including Shi'as, Ibadis, and Kharijites from southern Arabia and Persia—who sought refuge and new opportunities in East Africa. In the late thirteenth century, Shi'a communities along the Swahili coast claiming Shirazi origin (that is, from Shiraz, in Iran) were steadily replaced by those that were Sunni in orientation. Also during the thirteenth century, a group from Tashkent, in Central Asia, fleeing Mongol attacks, settled in Mogadishu. Another group, the Mahdalis, a prominent merchant family from Yemen, similarly relocated to the East African coast. While politics may have ultimately pushed these immigrants—and their particular brands of Islam—out of their homes, they were also drawn to the land, resources, and trading opportunities in East Africa.

Along much of the coast (as well as on the numerous islands off the mainland), farmers used the narrow strip of fertile, agriculturally productive land to grow both staple crops and spices. Abundant mangrove poles along the shore, as well as highly prized ivory and gold from the interior (the latter largely from Zimbabwe via the seaport of Sofala, located on the southern coast of Mozambique), were of even greater interest to merchants. Alongside these commodities and luxury items was a growing trade in slaves—captives of war—who were used for agricultural labor in Yemen (coffee) and Oman (dates), pearl diving in the Persian Gulf, and domestic labor in the Ottoman Empire. The combination of goods and labor made the coast attractive to several waves of settlers, the Omani among them. As a result, the size of Muslim settlements from the Arabian Peninsula to the Swahili coast grew steadily between the thirteenth and fifteenth centuries. By that time, farther to the north, on the Ethiopian side of the Red Sea, the inhabitants of the important coastal towns of Aydhab and Sawakin also had adopted Islam.

Although trade largely drove the process of Islamization in East Africa, war between Ethiopian Muslims and Ethiopian Christians saw a temporary expansion of Muslim political authority inland in the early sixteenth century. The Somalian imam Ahmad Ibn Ibrahim al-Ghazi, of the coastal Adal sultanate, led the Muslims in their *jihad* (armed resistance, or struggle of the lower order, as opposed to the struggle to get closer to Allah through other, spiritual means). For fourteen years, the Adal sultanate ruled most of the Christian Ethiopian territories. In 1543, when Ahmad was killed, his widow, Bati Del Wanbara, briefly maintained Adal rule, but the Christians soon regained their land. Throughout the war, trade continued, including the slave trade. Both prior to and long after the conflict, thousands of East Africans (Ethiopians, Sudanese, and Nubians) were captured, sold into slavery, and shipped to Muslim-controlled ports in Arabia, the Persian Gulf, and western India.

The life of one of Ethiopia's most notable forced migrants, Malik Ambar (Document 25), provides a way of understanding the interconnectivity of Islam, trade, and military slavery in East Africa and South Asia. Born in Ethiopia in approximately 1548, Ambar was enslaved and sold in Mocha (in Yemen). From there he was taken to Baghdad, where he received an education from his slave master, Mir Qasim. In the 1570s, he was resold and taken to the Deccan, where he served a fellow Abyssinian, Malik Dabir, who had risen through the ranks in the Ahmednagar sultanate. Following Dabir's death, Ambar left the area for the neighboring sultanate of Bijapur. He returned to Ahmednagar after building a cavalry of his own. By 1600, he had several thousand warriors under his command and had installed himself as regent minister (the prime minister and often de facto ruler of a sultanate), a position he held until his death in 1626. Though born a non-Muslim, he had become an adherent of Islam. His life story helps demonstrate both the Africanization of Islam and the extent to which Islam had become part of the Indian Ocean world.

SOUTH ASIA: DELHI, THE DECCAN, AND MALABAR

Islam originally reached Sind (the area bordering northwestern India) in the early eighth century through Arab conquest, but it was not until the thirteenth century that it began to have a more visible presence in India's interior. The process of Islamization in northern India was almost exclusively led by Central Asian Turkic and Persian Muslims who established themselves politically over the majority Hindu population. Because of the demographic imbalance, Islam accommodated a variety of perspectives, people, and traditions, leading to new forms of syncretism, cultural syntheses, and pluralism.

Also in the early eighth century, Muslim Arab merchants settled on the Malabar Coast of southwest India, helping to link al-Hind (the Arabic name for India) to seaborne trade routes. These Muslims, known as the Mappila, lived under Hindu monarchs, married local women, and developed a culture of their own, fusing southern Arabian customs with those long established by Hindus along the coast, including the practice of inheritance following both maternal and paternal lines.

While Muslims continued to trade and form communities in this area, it was not until the establishment of the first Turkic dynasty in Delhi under the Mamluk ruler Qutb ud-din Aibak in the early thirteenth century that Islam became a discernible presence in northern India. In contrast to Malabar, Persian, not Arabic, conventions came to dominate northern Indian courts. Over the next six hundred years, the language of the Muslim elite there was Persian. During that time, however, Urdu, a popular language based on the Khariboli dialect of Delhi, came into being and became famous for its use in poetry. Using Arabic script, Urdu combined the structure of Sanskrit with Persian, Arabic, Turkic, and Hindi words. Over time, Urdu became the lingua franca among Muslims in the subcontinent, with local variants evolving, such as Dakhini, spoken in the western Deccan.

During the late thirteenth and fourteenth centuries, a succession of Persianized Muslim Turko-Afghan regimes, collectively known as the Delhi sultanate, came to dominate politics in northern India. Like the multiple invaders preceding them, these Turks and Afghans originally entered the subcontinent through the Khyber Pass, winding through the rugged northwestern mountains connecting modern-day Afghanistan and Pakistan—a critical point in the Silk Road. Their primary aim was to secure the agricultural surplus of the northern countryside, although they occasionally made incursions into the south. The leaders of the sultanate would give rights to a share of the revenue from the land under their control to compensate their subordinates.

These dynasties brought practical innovations with them, including new cropping patterns, irrigation techniques, and mounted warfare, all of which made their way into the Deccan. Attuned to both urban development and rural growth—largely to sustain the urban centers, patronize their artisans and scholars, maintain their armies, and otherwise support their courts—the Delhi sultanate built extensive road networks, which stimulated and supported trade throughout the region and provided access to the markets of the wider Indian Ocean world.[18]

The sultanate's urban and rural development, along with its maintenance of ethnically diverse courts and religiously pluralistic governance, resulted in customs and patterns that continued under the Mughals of the north and the Deccan kingdoms of central India. Like the Muslim-led polities that followed, the Delhi sultanate was not exclusively Islamic. It did not engage in jihad, and its rulers were not religious leaders. Hindu culture permeated its courts, with Hindu officials often holding high posts. Like other rulers of the period and region, its sultans were expected to patronize different religious institutions. They funded the ulema as well as the spiritual guides of the Muslim community, the Sufi *shaykhs*. Throughout the sultanate, Sufi teachings, including the most important traditions—Chishti, Qadiri, Suhrawardiyya, and Naqshbandi, all of which were either Central or West Asian in origin—developed alongside South Asian Hindu traditions of spiritual discipline and devotion.

The Delhi sultanate's ethnic pluralism was evident among its rulers and their courts, which included a combination of Turkic, Afghan, Persian, and indigenous Indians. Others were also sometimes present in their courts, including the Moroccan qadi Ibn Battuta (Document 1).[19]

While the rulers were Muslim, its subjects were overwhelmingly non-Muslim—mostly Hindu. In a pattern distinct from Muslim rule elsewhere in Dar al-Islam (lands under Muslim political authority), Hindus were designated as *dhimmis* and were left to their own laws and customs. Although *dhimmis* were subject to the per capita tax called the *jizyah*, they were exempt from military service.

The Delhi sultan Muhammad bin Tughluq, in whose court Ibn Battuta served, was particularly open and interested in expanding the intellectual and religious frontiers of his kingdom. He brought in dozens of talented foreigners to serve in his administration and judiciary, rewarding them with large gifts and stipends. He also invited Hindus and Jains (followers of an ancient religion in India that teaches spiritual liberation through nonviolence and material renunciation) to engage in theological debate. More than any other ruler of the sultanate, Tughluq pressed most successfully southward, establishing Deogiri (Daulatabad) in the Deccan, about four hundred miles south of the imperial seat. Some twenty years later, a Turkic-Afghan officer named Zafar Khan (also known as Bahman Shah) led a revolt against the sultanate and founded the Bahmani sultanate in the Deccan. Around the same time, the Hindu kingdom of Vijayanagar, based in southern India, was founded by brothers who had served the northern sultanate. Although the brothers were Muslim at one time, they had become strong adherents of the Hindu god Shiva, sharply distinguishing themselves from the predominantly Muslim-ruled Delhi and Bahmani sultanates, and pointing to the fluidity of Hinduism and Islam in South Asia.

In 1526, the Delhi sultanate fell to the Mughal forces of the Central Asian Zahir al-Din Muhammad Babur at the Battle of Panipat, just northwest of Delhi. While Babur's victory marked the end of the sultanate, it is his grandson Akbar who is the most famous Mughal. During his nearly fifty-year reign (1556–1605), Akbar pushed Mughal frontiers north to Kabul and Kashmir, east to Bengal and coastal Orissa, and southwest to Rajasthan and Gujarat, as well as to the northern part of the Deccan, where several smaller sultanates replaced Bahmani rule. He also continued the policy of encouraging diverse and inclusive rule, incorporating powerful indigenous lineages, notably the Rajputs, into the sultanate. The Rajputs maintained their own rights to revenues in their domains. The Mughals began the dynastic custom of marrying Rajput women, who were not expected to convert to Islam. Mughal elites comprised an even more diverse mix than the Delhi sultanate: They included not only different peoples from Central Asia but also Persians, Arabs, Rajputs, Brahmins (upper-caste Hindus), and, later, Marathas (southern Hindus).

Akbar, who was born a Sunni but had been exposed favorably to Shi'ism growing up, was open to a range of views in his court, where he welcomed Sufis, Hindus, Jains, Jesuits (a Catholic order), and Zoroastrians (adherents of a Persian-based monotheistic religion) (Document 36).

By the mid-seventeenth century, the Mughals had become the most powerful empire on the Indian subcontinent. They reached the farthest and accelerated the processes of urban and rural development that had begun under previous rulers. They were wealthier and controlled significantly larger populations than the Ottoman Turks and Persian Safavids, contemporary Muslim-ruled empires in the Middle East, with whom they had much in common culturally.

Although Akbar's rule reached across half of India, he was never able to conquer the Deccan, in large part because of the diplomatic and military maneuverings of Malik Ambar. Only after Ambar died were the Mughals, under Akbar's grandson Shah Jahan, able to take over the central Indian plateau. In addition to his territorial expansion, Akbar's most heralded legacy was his openness to other religious traditions and influences. The emperor even developed a syncretic religion called Din-i-ilahi (Divine Faith), which incorporated certain aspects of Hinduism, Jainism, Christianity, and Zoroastrianism into Islam. Although Akbar's new religion did not continue beyond his lifetime, his great-grandson Dara Shikoh advocated for a kind of pantheism that was equally open to other religious faiths and practices and blatantly heterodox (Document 38). Declared a *murtad* (apostate), Shikoh was executed by his brother and political rival Aurangzeb, the future Mughal emperor.

Even as politics played out in imperial India, Islam in South Asia, unlike that in most areas of the Indian Ocean world, was advanced through cooperation between Sufis and local ulema. Sufi poetry and songs were used as ways of teaching new adherents the basic tenets of the religion, although some Sufi poetry, such as Amir Khusraw's *ghazals* (devotional poems in the form of songs), pushed well beyond the boundaries of orthodox Islam (Document 35). Indeed, a range of expressions of Islam flourished in South Asia, where, beginning at least as early as the twelfth century, Delhi, Deccan, and Bengal-based Muslim rulers patronized sculptors, architects, and painters who drew on Hindu- and Jain-inspired art and architecture.[20] By virtue of their largely urban locations—where Muslims were most prominent—Buddhists in India were more substantially affected by the spread of Islam than people of other faiths. Also, as with many other non-Muslims across the Indian Ocean world, Buddhists were known to adopt Islam in order to remain competitive with Muslim merchants. Hindus, by contrast, were mostly agriculturalists and therefore less affected by the religious influence of Muslims, with whom they had less contact.

Merchants in Gujarat, the Malabar Coast of western India, and Sri Lanka established Muslim enclaves at Cambay, Mangalore, Calicut, Cochin, Quilon, Puttalam, and Colombo. The merchants, and the coastal communities they joined, became wealthy, exporting cotton, tea, cinnamon, cloves, nutmeg, and black pepper, while importing luxury items such as Arabian horses and African ivory. These coastal Muslim communities remained culturally distinct from their inland coreligionists. And although these communities shared common traits of maritime life and religious identity, they were themselves diverse. Both Sunni and Shi'a Muslims lived along the coast. Among the Shi'a, there were two major Isma'ili subgroups: Bohras, who had ties to communities in Yemen, and Khojas, who were known for incorporating local Hindu symbols and practices into their worship. Sayyids—those who claimed to be descendants of the Prophet Muhammad—were especially influential in bringing Islam and Muslim prestige to coastal communities.[21]

In addition to the blending of cultural and artistic forms and the creation of new languages and dialects, Muslims in India extended *dhimmi* status to Hindus and Buddhists, while upholding the Hindu caste system. The extension of *dhimmi* status to non-monotheists (highly unorthodox by Middle Eastern standards) and the replication of the existing caste system illustrate the development of Islam in South Asia, where the faith was Asianized, in the same way that it was Africanized as Africans came into the religion. As people from across the Indian Ocean world brought their particular sensibilities, traditions, and daily practices to Islam, the result was an ever-widening and ever more complex *ummah*.

SOUTHEAST ASIA: SUMATRA, MALACCA, AND ACEH

The adoption of Islam into Southeast Asia was not widespread until the fourteenth century, although a few Arab Muslims made their way into the region as early as the eighth century. Over the next centuries, they were followed by a small but steady stream of Muslims from southern Arabia and western India. The earliest waves of Muslim migrants into Southeast Asia formed enclaves among the region's predominantly Hindu and Buddhist populations. They were joined in the late ninth century by Chinese Muslims, many of whom had been expelled from Canton. Sufi missionaries came next, in the eleventh century. Lastly, Muslim Indians, following in the footsteps of Hindus and Buddhists from southern India several centuries earlier, reached Southeast Asia beginning in the late twelfth century.[22]

With thirteenth-century advancements in maritime technology, Muslim migration into Southeast Asia accelerated. While Muslim Arab navigators relied on the *kamal*, a wooden rectangle attached to a knotted string to measure the height of the North Star, the invention of the Chinese floating compass made navigation possible even when the stars were not visible. With such advancements came increasing numbers of Muslim migrants and the adoption of Islam by local communities. In the thirteenth century, Samudera, located on the northern coast of Sumatra, became the first port city in Southeast Asia to adopt Islam (Document 29). Muslim settlements in Sumatra were followed by those in Java, the Malay Peninsula, Borneo, Celebes (Sulawesi), the Maluku islands, and finally the southern Philippines.

Although Muslims reached the shores of Southeast Asia within the first two centuries of the founding of Islam, the first two Muslim states there, Sumatra and Java, were not organized until the fourteenth and fifteenth centuries, respectively. Malacca, located on the southern side of the Malay Peninsula, became a hub for Muslim traders and missionaries. Even though Malacca's ruler converted to Islam in the fifteenth century, pre-Islamic spiritual and Hindu practices continued at both the highest levels of power and among the city's general population (Document 33). The fifteenth-century Omani navigator Ahmad Ibn Majid was especially harsh in his condemnation of Malacca's Muslims for not following what he viewed as proper Islamic conventions (Document 6). In Southeast Asia, as elsewhere in the Indian Ocean littoral (coastal region), trade combined with politics and drove migration and the subsequent adoption of Islam alongside existing indigenous religious practices.

The initial rapid growth of Malacca from a small fishing port in the late fourteenth century into one of the Indian Ocean's most important Muslim trading centers (Document 3) was the result of the rulers of Malacca implementing competitive customs rates and using Chinese naval protection against piracy. Malacca's customs rates did not necessarily favor Muslims but yielded a significant increase in trade and population. The bustling port city, like those across much of the Indian Ocean world, was multiethnic, attracting South Asians (including Muslims from the Coromandel Coast, Bengal, and Gujarat), as well as Javanese and

Chinese traders, many of whom were Muslim. Especially influential in Malacca were Gujaratis, who traded various commodities, notably cotton from the port of Cambay for pepper from Malacca.

Just as Malacca was on the rise, imperial China launched a series of extraordinary expeditions across the Indian Ocean. Beginning in 1405, and continuing over the next two and a half decades, the Ming emperor Chengzu (a.k.a. Zhu Di) charged his grand eunuch, an ethnic Hui Muslim named Zheng He, with the task of leading several voyages across the Western Ocean, the Chinese name for the eastern portion of the Indian Ocean (Document 3). With a mix of commercial, political, and scientific purposes in mind, Zheng He's fleets, consisting of several hundred of the largest ships to set sail across the ocean, also helped to suppress piracy in the Strait of Malacca. Linking China to the extensive Muslim maritime networks of the wider Indian Ocean, which stretched from the shores of Southeast Asia to East Africa's Swahili coast, Zheng He's fleets reached as far as Malindi in 1415.

China's eminence on the high seas would help Malacca flourish, with naval protection offered in exchange for tribute. However, Ming China's maritime presence in Southeast Asia was short-lived; its overseas program was abandoned in 1433 due to a combination of internal political disputes and economic troubles.[23] Nevertheless, both Malacca and Islam continued to thrive in the region. Indeed, Malacca became the most important trading center of the region, establishing close ties with both Hindu Tamil and Muslim Gujarati merchants. Trade was the principal way in which Muslims gained prominence across much of the Indian Ocean littoral, but Southeast Asian Muslims occasionally launched military attacks on non-Muslims to take control of trade routes.

Writing of the importance of Malacca, the Portuguese observer Tomé Pires (Document 8) noted at the beginning of the sixteenth century that the port of "Cambay chiefly stretches out two arms, with her right arm she reaches towards Aden and with the other towards Malacca."[24] Although merchants continued to conduct business in Malacca throughout the century, the Aceh sultanate, located at the northern tip of Sumatra, soon took over as Southeast Asia's principal trading hub. From Aceh, Muslim merchants made their way to Cambay, which was supplanted by the nearby port of Surat by the end of the sixteenth century when its harbor succumbed to the buildup of silt. Surat's products were in turn carried to Aden and points beyond.[25]

As people, products, and religious practices were introduced into Southeast Asia through trade, the Arab language increasingly served as a unifying force. Arabic words and script infused the languages of the Malay Peninsula, Sumatra, and Java, bringing commonality among Muslim traders and their communities in this easternmost part of the *ummah*. But the linguistic influence went both ways. Just as Southeast Asian languages were Arabicized, Arabic was vernacularized, with the spelling, pronunciation, and meaning of Arabic words often changing when adopted into local languages.[26] And so it was with Islam, as foreign Muslims and their cultures were absorbed into local Southeast Asian populations.

Beginning in the fourteenth century, Muslim merchants, scholars, and pilgrims traveled more regularly across the expanse of the Indian Ocean. Among the most notable Muslims to travel from Southeast Asia to Arabia was the Sumatran-born Sufi Abd al-Ra'uf of Singkel. Like his Hajji predecessor Ibn Battuta three centuries earlier, who began his long journey to Mecca from the western end of the *ummah*, Abd al-Ra'uf set out from the eastern end, in approximately 1640. Studying the Qur'an and Hadith in Medina under the Kurdish scholar Shaykh Ibrahim al-Kurani, the Sumatran subsequently traveled to Yemen before returning to the Hijaz and becoming a teacher himself. Abd al-Ra'uf spent nearly twenty years in Mecca teaching hundreds of Indonesians who traveled to Arabia, many of whom he initiated into the Shattariyya Sufi order, of which he was a distinguished member. In 1661, Abd al-Ra'uf returned to Sumatra, settling in Aceh, where he taught for another three decades. There he received hundreds of Javanese pilgrims en route to Arabia and helped bring many other Southeast Asians into Islam (Document 34).[27]

Between 1641 and 1699, four Muslim women ruled Aceh. Most notable among them was Sultana Taj al-Alam Safiyat al-Din Shah (r. 1641–1675), whose father, Iskandar Muda Shah, was a renowned leader and diplomat. Known for her great patronage of artists and scholars, Safiyat al-Din Shah's sponsorship led to Acehnese displacing Malay as the language of state and the arts. However, the female sultans' collective reign was marked by strife, as they were forced to fend off multiple internal political attacks. As elsewhere in the Indian Ocean world, patriarchal forms of governance ultimately came to dominate. Still, a number of matriarchal pre-Islamic customs were maintained and incorporated into Muslim societies in Southeast Asia. For instance, both lineage and inheritance continued to be traced through women in western Sumatra, despite the widespread Muslim convention of patriarchal descent and inheritance in the region.[28]

The dialectical nature of religion as a cultural and social product ultimately based on power is evident in the spread of Islam in Southeast

Asia. Religious beliefs, rituals, and practices, being inextricably tied to culture and society, were effectively remixed into new forms of life that transformed all involved, albeit at different levels of intensity and in different periods of time. Sometimes the changes were immediate; other times they took place over the course of generations. As Islam came into East Africa, South Asia, and Southeast Asia, cultures and societies were transformed, just as Islam itself was transformed. This ongoing process of cultural synthesis was centuries in the making across the Indian Ocean world.

CONCLUSION

Between the twelfth and seventeenth centuries, Muslims of different backgrounds plied the Indian Ocean or traveled overland, bringing a wide range of people, products, and ideas into contact with one another. Across this world, Islam thrived. Traveling Muslims transformed the cultures and people with whom they made contact while continuously diversifying the *ummah* itself. Through a combination of social interaction, settlement, and marriage, Muslims not only altered the societies comprising the ever-growing *ummah* but transformed what it meant to be Muslim. In these ways, Islam would come to reflect the beliefs, practices, and traditions of local populations across the Indian Ocean world.

Islam initially spread across much of the Middle East and North Africa relatively quickly through military force. By the early eighth century, Muslims reached the Iberian Peninsula to the west and Sind to the east. Early Muslim military expansion in the Middle East either opened up or extended trading opportunities, which in turn led to the religious expansion of Islam into areas under Muslim political control. Over the subsequent four centuries, Muslim merchants spread Islam and its cultural traits to port towns and cities along the rim of the Indian Ocean— down the Swahili coast of East Africa, to Gujarat and the Malabar Coast of western India, and to parts of Southeast Asia. In time, Islam reached farther inland as sovereigns, from local sultans to emperors, adopted the faith and lent their financial resources to Islamic intellectual, artistic, and cultural developments.

Beyond Arabia, Muslim expansion first spread along the western portion of the ocean, from Sofala in East Africa to Calicut in southern India. By the twelfth century, Islam reached clear across the eastern portion of the ocean to Southeast Asia, gaining a firmer footing in Indonesia by the early fifteenth century. Merchants, traveling on dhows propelled by the seasonal monsoons and ocean currents, led the process of Islam's adoption by local populations through example, proselytization, and marriage. Merchants were followed by Sufis and scholars, who in successive waves brought the message of a single, compassionate god to the Indian Ocean littoral and across the interior. Although the Qur'an and Hadith remained primary sources of guidance for those who adopted Islam, local traditions, customary laws, and existing social practices were variously incorporated into the faith. The presence of Muslims could be seen and heard in the languages, dress, music, architecture, and poetry of the growing *ummah*.

By the seventeenth century, there were as many Muslims living outside the Middle East as there were within the Arab heartlands. Across the Indian Ocean world, the minarets of mosques dotted the skylines of Muslim cities—large and small—while the *Azzan*, the call to prayer, filled the air of Muslim cities and enclaves alike. To be sure, Muslims in the Indian Ocean world were extremely diverse—from the navigator Zheng He and the regent minister Malik Ambar to the Sufi scholar Abd al-Ra'uf and the female sultan Taj al-Alam Safiyat al-Din Shah. They and their non-Muslim neighbors—including observers such as the Italian explorer Marco Polo (Document 2), the French doctor François Bernier (Document 11), and the Dutch traveler Pieter van den Broecke (Document 25)—comprised a multifaceted and multilayered Islamic world.

Notwithstanding some of the basic tenets of equality and fairness in Islamic teachings, a social hierarchy emerged within the *ummah*, with Arab Muslims considering themselves essentially superior to non-Arab Muslims. Muslim Arabs, followed by Persians, tended to fashion themselves as purer Muslims than Muslim East Africans or South and Southeast Asians. Not only did they see themselves as literally closer to the origins of Islam in Mecca and Medina, but they also perceived the incorporation of non-Arab cultural elements into Islam as either a corruption or a dilution of the religion.

Even during the Prophet's lifetime, there was no absolute consensus on what Islam was or how it should be practiced, as Muhammad was constantly offering answers to new questions and guidance in new circumstances. Islam was evolving then and continued to evolve after Muhammad died. Following his death, some Muslims attempted to claim, in a definitive way, what was Islamic or not. But as the great tenth-century Muslim Persian historian al-Tabari made plain by including references and sources with contradictory accounts of events in the early formation of the *ummah*, there are indeed multiple ways of understanding words and actions based on context and point of view.

The attempt to impose a fixed set of interpretations and customs on what Islam is by ulema or anyone else, is like telling the tides to stop rising or the winds from blowing. One may attempt to interpret Islam in everlasting fashion, but people and their societies do not stand still, and any attempt to define Islam based solely on readings of the Qur'an or the Hadith ultimately distorts who Muslims are and what they have been doing in practice since the initial formation of the *ummah*. Differences within the ever-changing *ummah* grew in proportion to Islam's expansion beyond western Arabia. As the fourteenth-century observer Ibn Battuta variously notes in his *Rihala (Travels)*, Muslims shaped — and were themselves shaped by — the fluid and heterogeneous character of Islam as it spread throughout the Indian Ocean world (Document 1).

Whether Hindu, Buddhist, Jain, Zoroastrian, Christian, Jewish, or having practiced some kind of ancestral veneration, spiritualism, polytheism, or combination thereof, people across the Indian Ocean world became Muslim for a variety of reasons. While many people became Muslim as a matter of genuine faith, others pragmatically adopted Islamic identities to gain access to Muslims' extensive trade networks or for political purposes. Still others became Muslim for the prestige increasingly associated with Islamic civilization, including its legal and philosophical traditions (Documents 7, 13, 15, 17, 19, 36, 40, and 41). Most new adherents continued to follow some aspects of their existing religious traditions alongside more-commonly accepted Muslim practices. In time, millions of people in the Indian Ocean world adopted Islam in their own way and passed on a more heterogeneous version of Islam to their families and communities.

To give expression to this rich and dynamic history of Islam in the Indian Ocean world, the documents in this book cover the period from the time when there was a discernible Muslim presence across much of the Indian Ocean world (at the beginning of the twelfth century) to the time just before the rise of European power in the region (at the end of the seventeenth century). Included are both traditional written sources — religious texts (Documents 18 and 19), letters (Documents 16 and 37), travel accounts (Documents 1–4, 6, 11, 22, and 27), government and business records (Document 26) — and stories that were passed down through oral traditions, from popular folktales, such as *The Thousand and One Nights* (Document 10), to Sufi poetry (Document 35) and women's devotional work songs (Document 31).

From East Africa to Southeast Asia, the process of Muslim expansion and adoption consisted of both the Islamization of the Indian Ocean world and the Afro-Asianization of Islam (Documents 20–22). With increasing numbers of people and traditions incorporated into the *ummah*, notions of who was a Muslim and what constituted Islam were regularly challenged and changed over time. The centuries-long process was fluid and dynamic. Never simply a matter of a static set of ideals or concepts (with accompanying rules and regulations) imposed on others without reactions or responses, Islam was reconfigured by each new generation of Muslims. From all ranks, races, ethnicities, and backgrounds, people across the region made and remade Islam as their own.

How people transformed Islam and the Indian Ocean world over time is a lesson in world history that stretches across many centuries, a vast ocean, and the plains, valleys, mountains, deserts, and riverbanks of this wide and encompassing region. Although the analysis of this process begins in western Arabia, the following collection of documents reveals a distinctly southern and eastern purview: into East Africa, South Asia, and Southeast Asia. This volume is, in part, a response to growing scholarly attention being paid to premodern forms of globalization and an increased interest in trying to better understand Islam in a larger geographical and historical context—that is, beyond the Arab Middle East. Exploring the simultaneous Islamization of the Indian Ocean world and Afro-Asianization of Islam through documents from the twelfth through the seventeenth century, and from a range of voices and perspectives, is one way of doing so. It is also an invitation to bear witness to an earlier, extended moment in the expansion and transformation of Islam in the Indian Ocean world.

NOTES

[1] For an articulation of the concept of Africanization, see David Robinson, *Muslim Societies in African History* (Cambridge: Cambridge University Press, 2004), 27, and John Parker and Richard Rathbone, *African History: A Very Short Introduction* (New York: Oxford University Press, 2003), 75. Such articulations should be understood as heuristic ways of characterizing what are highly heterogeneous and culturally porous geographic areas of the world since neither "Africa" nor "Asia" are homogeneous or contained, culturally or otherwise. See Roman Loimeier, *Muslim Societies in Africa: A Historical Anthropology* (Bloomington: Indiana University Press, 2014), 18.

[2] *Ethiopia* is a term used in historical texts to describe the people and nations within the Horn of Africa. It is also referred to as *Abyssinia*, and its people and their descendants are called *Abyssinians*.

[3] In addition to interacting with Jews and Christians, Muhammad moved in Hanifiyyah circles in Arabia (Hanifism being the belief in an unadulterated form of Abrahamic monotheism). See Reza Aslan, *No God, but God: The Origins, Evolution, and Future of Islam* (New York: Random House, 2005), 14.

[4] I use *Hadith* to denote both the recorded sayings and the practices (Sunna) of the Prophet Muhammad. Among the six major Hadith collections, the most widely used is *Sahih al-Bukhari*, collected by the ninth-century Persian scholar Muhammad Ibn Isma'il al-Bukhari. See *Sahih al-Bukhari*, trans. Muhammad Muhsin Khan (Riyadh: Maktaba Dar-us-Salam, 1994).

[5] Legend holds that during the early seventh century, Sa'ad Ibn Abi Waqqas, the maternal uncle of the Prophet Muhammad, headed a Muslim delegation to China to meet the

emperor, whose admiration for Islam led to the building of China's first mosque. See Jonathan N. Lipman, *Familiar Strangers: A History of Muslims in Northwest China* (Seattle: University of Washington Press, 1997), 24–25.

[6]The Indian Ocean comprises several seas (e.g., Arabian, Red, and Andaman), gulfs (e.g., Aden, Persian, Oman, and Cambay), bays (e.g., Bengal and Arugam), channels (e.g., Mozambique and Kardiva), and straits (e.g., Madagascar, Malacca, and Bab-al-Mandeb). See Michael Pearson, *The Indian Ocean* (New York: Routledge, 2003), 16, and Abdul Sheriff, *Dhow Cultures of the Indian Ocean: Cosmopolitanism, Commerce, and Islam* (New York: Columbia University Press, 2010), 1–23.

[7]Edward Alpers describes the formation of such societies as "the evolution of hybrid cultures and cosmopolitan communities" in *The Indian Ocean in World History* (New York: Oxford University Press, 2014), 11.

[8]Ibn Battuta, *The Travels of Ibn Battuta*, trans. H. A. R. Gibb (Cambridge: Hakluyt, 1958), 1:229.

[9]Michael N. Pearson, "Merchants and States," in *The Political Economy of Merchant Empires*, ed. James D. Tracey (Cambridge: Cambridge University Press, 1991), 62.

[10]Sahih al-Bukhari, vol. 3, book 12, Hadith, 2139.

[11]Patricia Risso, *Merchants and Faith: Muslim Commerce and Culture in the Indian Ocean* (Boulder, Colo.: Westview Press, 1995), 19–20.

[12]Letter from Mahruz ben Jacob to his brother-in-law Abu Zikri ha-Kohen, quoted in Roxani Eleni Margariti, *Aden and the Indian Ocean Trade: 150 Years in the Life of a Medieval Arabian Port* (Chapel Hill: University of North Carolina Press, 2007), 157.

[13]Risso, *Merchants and Faith*, 70.

[14]Ibn Battuta, *The Travels of Ibn Battuta*, trans. H. A. R. Gibb (New Delhi: Goodword Books, 1929).

[15]Omar H. Ali, "The African Diaspora in the Indian Ocean World," exhibition, Schomburg Center for Research in Black Culture, New York Public Library, 2011, http://exhibitions.nypl.org/africansindianocean/index2.php.

[16]For a detailed discussion of this two-way process, see Robinson, *Muslim Societies in African History*, 27–59.

[17]Basil Davidson, *Africa in History: Themes and Outlines* (New York: Collier, 1974), 165.

[18]Barbara D. Metcalf and Thomas R. Metcalf, *A Concise History of India* (Cambridge: Cambridge University Press, 2006), 5.

[19]Ross E. Dunn, *The Adventures of Ibn Battuta: A Muslim Traveler of the Fourteenth Century* (Berkeley: University of California Press, 2005), 189.

[20]Barbara D. Metcalf, ed., *Islam in South Asia in Practice* (Princeton, N.J.: Princeton University Press, 2009), 14–15.

[21]Sheriff, *Dhow Cultures of the Indian Ocean*, 126.

[22]Among the physical evidence of the early Islamic presence in the region are Muslim gravestones in eastern Java. See Ronit Ricci, *Islam Translated: Literature, Conversion, and the Arabic Cosmopolis of South and Southeast Asia* (Chicago: University of Chicago Press, 2011), 5.

[23]Risso, *Merchants and Faith*, 48–49.

[24]Tomé Pires, *Suma Oriental of Tomé Pires: An Account of the East, from the Red Sea to China, Written in Malacca and India in 1512–1515*, ed. Armando Cortesão (London: Hakluyt Society, 1944), 1:41.

[25]Risso, *Merchants and Faith*, 94–95.

[26]Ricci, *Islam Translated*, 16.

[27]Azyumardi Azra, *The Origins of Islamic Reformism in Southeast Asia: Networks of Malay-Indonesian and Middle Eastern "Ulama" in the Seventeenth and Eighteenth Centuries* (Honolulu: University of Hawai'i Press, 2004), 70–81.

[28]Anthony Reid, ed., *Southeast Asia in the Early Modern Era: Trade, Power, and Belief* (Ithaca, N.Y.: Cornell University Press, 1993), 131.

PART TWO

The Documents

1

Ibn Battuta, Marco Polo, and Zheng He

Ibn Battuta, Marco Polo, and Zheng He—indefatigable explorers of the Indian Ocean world—offer three perspectives spanning from the late thirteenth century through the early fifteenth century. These accounts point to the widespread presence of Muslim merchants and Islam itself, as it was variously understood and practiced, across the vast region. Each of these narratives, written down by others, provides a snapshot of the period, with Ibn Battuta's being by far the most detailed.

1

IBN BATTUTA

The Travels of Ibn Battuta

ca. 1350

Ibn Battuta was a fourteenth-century Moroccan qadi who traveled across much of the Indian Ocean world starting in 1325. His recollections from more than a quarter-century of travel—including to Arabia, East Africa, India, and Southeast Asia—were written down by the literary scholar Ibn Juzayy. Ibn Battuta's Rihala (Travels) provides the most detailed account of the region during the premodern era, revealing a largely Islamic world that was multiracial, multiethnic, and interconnected. Following are excerpts from what he observed regarding merchants, long-distance trade, conditions at sea, pirates, religious practice, and gender relations. As you read the document, consider how Ibn Battuta viewed the different

Ibn Battuta, *The Travels of Ibn Battuta*, trans. H. A. R. Gibb, 4 vols. (Cambridge: Hakluyt, 1958–1994), 1:25–27, 227–30, 236, 260; 2:234, 374, 383–84; 3:393; 4:813–14, 826, 829–31, 856, 876–77, 911–12.

expressions of Islam in this region. Was he neutral in his observations, or did he express moral judgments?

[In 1329, early in his travels, Ibn Battuta left Jeddah, on the west coast of Arabia along the Red Sea, aboard an Abyssinian ship to continue his travels to the south and then to cut east across the Arabian Sea in the western Indian Ocean. He was near Oman when he wrote the following.]

My food during those days on that ship was dried dates and fish. Every morning and evening [the sailors] used to catch fish. . . . They used to cut them in pieces, broil them and give every person on the ship a portion, showing no preference to anyone over another, not even to the master of the vessel nor to any other, and they would eat them with dried dates. I had with me some bread and biscuit. . . . And when these were exhausted I had to live on those fish with the rest of them. . . .

[Travel by sea was always risky. The weather could change abruptly. In 1329, he described the reaction of one pilgrim when a violent storm blew in as they left the coast of Oman.]

There were accompanying us in the vessel a pilgrim [who] knew the Qur'an by heart and could write excellently. When he saw the storminess of the sea, he wrapped his head in a mantle that he had and pretended to sleep. When Allah gave us relief from what had befallen us, I said to him, "O Mawlana Khidr, what kind of thing did you see?" He replied, "When the storm came I kept my eyes open, watching to see whether the angels who receive men's souls had come. As I could not see them, I said, 'Praise be to Allah. If any of us were to be drowned, they could come to take the souls.' Then I would close my eyes and after a while open them again, to watch in the same manner, until Allah relieved us." . . .

[In 1331, Ibn Battuta traveled to the Swahili coast.]

After leaving Aden, I travelled by sea for four days and arrived at the town of Zeila. It is the capital of Berbera: the inhabitants are black and follow the Shafi'i rite. The country is a desert which stretches for two months' march, starting at Zeila and finishing at Mogadishu. Their beasts of burden are camels, and they also possess sheep which are famous for their butter. The people are dark-skinned and very many of them are heretics.

Zeila is a large town with an important market; but it is one of the dirtiest towns in existence, vile and evil-smelling. The cause of the stench is the great quantity of fish which is brought there, as well as the blood of the camels which are slaughtered in the streets. When we were there, we preferred to spend the night on board, although the sea was rough, rather than in town, on account of its unpleasantness.

From there we sailed fifteen nights and arrived at Mogadishu, which is a very large town. The people have very many camels, and slaughter many hundreds every day. They have also many sheep. The merchants are wealthy, and manufacture a material which takes its name from the town which is exported to Egypt and elsewhere. . . .

When young men came on board the ship on which I was, one of them approached me. My companions said to him: "He is not one of the merchants: he is a lawyer." Then the young men called his companions and said: "This man is a guest of the Qadi." One of the Qadi's friends came among them, and he told him of this. The Qadi came down to the beach with some of his pupils and sent one on board to fetch me. Then I disembarked with my companions, and greeted the Qadi and his followers. He said to me: "In the name of Allah, let us go and greet the shaikh." "Who is the shaikh?" I asked and he replied: "The sultan." For it is their custom here to call the sultan "shaikh." I answered the Qadi: "I will visit him as soon as I have found lodging." He replied: "It is the custom here, whenever a lawyer, or a Sharif [someone who claims to be a descendant of the Prophet Muhammad] or holy man comes, that he should not go to his lodging until he has seen the sultan." So I did what I was asked in accordance with their custom. . . .

We stayed there for three days, and each day they brought us food three times a day, as is their custom. The fourth day, which was a Friday, the Qadi, his pupils and one of the wazirs[1] of the Shaikh came and brought me a suit of clothes. Their dress consists of a loin-cloth, which is fastened round the waist, instead of the drawers, of which they are ignorant. There was a tunic of Egyptian linen with a border, a cloak . . . and a fringed turban of Egyptian material. . . .

We went to the chief mosque, and prayed behind the *maqsurah*, the enclosure for the Shaikh. He replied with his good wishes for us both, and talked to the Qadi in the local language, and then said to the men in Arabic: "You are welcome: you have honored our country by coming

---

[1] "vizier," a high-ranking official.

and have rejoiced us." He went out into the courtyard of the mosque and stopped at the tomb of his son, which is there. He recited a passage from the Qur'an and prayed. Then came the wazirs . . . and the military commanders and greeted him. In doing this they observed the same customs as are followed in the Yemen. The man who gives his greeting places his forefinger on the ground, and then on his head, and says: "May Allah make you glorious!"

After that the Shaikh went out of the door of the mosque and put his sandals on. He ordered the Qadi and myself to do likewise, and set off on foot to his house, which is near the mosque, everyone else following barefoot. Over his head they carried a silk canopy, its four piles topped with a golden bird. He wore a sweeping cloak of green Jerusalem stuff, over clothes of Egyptian linen. He had a silk girdle and a large turban. In front of him they beat drums and played trumpets and oboes. He was preceded by the amirs of the army, and followed by the Qadi, the lawyers and the Sharifs.

With this ceremony he entered his audience hall. . . . This is their custom every Friday.

On Saturday the people come to the door of the Shaikh's house and sit on benches outside. The Qadi, the lawyers, the Sharifs, the holy men, the Shaikhs and those who have made the pilgrimage enter an outer room and sit on wooden benches arranged for that purpose. The Qadi sits on his bench alone, and each of these classes of person has its own bench, which is not shared with any other. The Shaikh then takes his place in his hall of audience, and sends for the Qadi. He takes his place on the Shaikh's left, and then the lawyers come in, and the chief of them sit in front of the Shaikh. The others greet the Shaikh and go back again. Then the Sharifs enter, and the chief of them sit before him: the remainder greet him and go back outside. But if they are guests of the Shaikh, they sit on his right hand. The same ceremonial is observed by persons of position and pilgrims, and then by the wazirs, the amirs and the military commanders, each rank by itself.

Then food is brought, and the Qadi, the Sharifs and those who are in the audience chamber eat in the presence of the Shaikh, and he with them. The rest eat in the refectory [dining hall]; there they observe the same procedure as that of their entering the Shaikh's audience chamber.

After this the Shaikh retires to his private apartments, and the Qadi, the wazirs, and the private secretary and four of the chiefs sit to hear the causes and complaints. Questions of religious law are decided by the Qadi: other cases are judged by the council, that is, the wazirs and amirs. If the case requires the views of the sultan, it is put in writing for him. He sends back an immediate reply, written on the back of the paper, as his discretion may decide. This has always been the custom among these people.

Then I set off by sea from the town of Mogadishu for the land of the Swahili and the town of Kilwa, which is in the land of the Zanj. We arrived at Mombasa, a large island two days' journey from the land of the Swahili. The island is quite separate from the mainland. It grows bananas, lemons and oranges. The people also gather a fruit which they call jamun which looks like an olive. It has a nut like an olive, but its taste is very sweet. The people do not engage in agriculture, but import grain from the Swahili. The greater part of their diet is bananas and fish. They follow the Shafi'i rite and are devout, chaste and virtuous.

Their mosques are very strongly constructed of wood. Beside the door of each mosque are one or two wells, one or two cubits [approximately forty inches total] deep. They draw water from them with a wooden vessel which is fixed on to the end of a thin stick a cubit long. The earth round the mosque and the well is stamped flat. Anyone who wishes to enter the mosque first washes his feet; beside the door is a piece of heavy material for drying them. Anyone who wishes to perform the ritual ablutions, takes the vessel between his thighs, pours water on his hands, and so makes his ablutions. Everyone here goes barefoot.

We spent a night on the island and set sail for Kilwa, the principal town on the coast, the greater part of whose inhabitants are Zanj of very black in complexion. Their faces are scarred. . . .

Kilwa is one of the most beautiful and well-constructed towns in the world. The whole of it is elegantly built, the roofs are built with mangrove poles. There is very much rain. The people are engaged in a holy war, for their country lies beside the pagan Zanj. The chief qualities are devotion and piety: they follow the Shafi'i rite. . . .

When I arrived, the sultan was Abu al-Muzaffar Hasan surnamed Abu al-Mawahib [the Father of Gifts] on account of his numerous charitable gifts. He frequently makes raids into the Zanj country, attacks them and carries off booty, of which he reserves a fifth, using it in the manner prescribed by the Qur'an. That reserved for the kinsfolk of the Prophet is kept separate in the Treasury, and when Sharifs come to visit him, he gives it them. They come to him from Iraq, the Hijaz, and other countries. I found several Sharifs from the Hijaz at his court. . . . This sultan is very humble; he sits and eats with beggars, and venerates holy men and descendants of the Prophet. . . .

It is the custom of the people of [Mogadishu] that, when a vessel reaches the anchorage, the *sumbuqs*, which are small boats, come out to it. In each *sumbuq* there are a number of young men of the town, each one of whom brings a covered platter containing food and presents it to one of the merchants on the ship, saying "This is my guest," and each of the others does the same. The merchant, on disembarking, goes only to the house of his host among the young men, except those who have made frequent journeys to the town and have gained some acquaintance with its inhabitants; these lodge where they please. When he takes up residence with his host, the latter sells his goods for him and buys for him; and if anyone buys anything from him at too low a price or sells to him in the absence of his host, that sale is held invalid by them. This practice is a profitable one for them. . . .

The population of Zafari [in southwest Oman] are engaged in trading, and have no livelihood except from this. It is their custom that when a vessel arrives from India or elsewhere, the sultan's slaves go down to the shore, and come out to the ship in a *sumbuq*, carrying with them a complete set of robes for the owner of the vessel or his agent, and also for the *rubban*, who is the captain, and for the *kirai,* who is the ship's writer. Three horses are brought for them, on which they mount [and proceed] with drums and trumpets playing before them from the seashore to the sultan's residence, where they make their salutations to the vizier. Hospitality is supplied to all who are in the vessel for three nights, and when the three nights are up they eat in the sultan's residence. These people do this in order to gain the goodwill of the shipowners. . . .

[Calicut, on India's Malabar Coast, had surpassed the port of Cambay, in Gujarat, as the most important link between East Africa and Southeast Asia. Here Ibn Battuta describes its importance in Indian Ocean trading networks.]

[Calicut] is one of the largest harbours in the world. It is visited by men from China, Sumatra, Ceylon, the Maldives, Yemen and Fars, and in it gather merchants from all quarters. . . . In all the lands of the Mulaybar [Malabar], except in this one land alone, it is the custom that whenever a ship is wrecked all that is taken from it belongs to the treasury. At Calicut however it is retained by its owners and for that reason Calicut has become a flourishing city and attracts large numbers of merchants. . . .

[At Calicut, Ibn Battuta saw a range of ships—from Yemen, southern Iran, the Maldives, Sri Lanka, and Java—and various conditions on board. He was most impressed by the massive Chinese junks. The largest of these ships carried up to six hundred sailors as well as four hundred

archers and other soldiers; each of their oars was worked by up to fifteen
men at a time. He describes one of the junks he sailed on.]

. . . It has cabins, suites and salons for merchants; a set of rooms and a
latrine; it can be locked by its occupant, and he can take along with him
slave-girls and wives. Often a man will live in his suite unknown to any of
the others on board until they meet on reaching some town. The sailors
have their children living on board ship, and they cultivate green stuffs,
vegetables, and ginger in wooden tanks. The owner's factor on board
ship is like a great *amir*.

[In the early 1340s, the Moroccan faced a harrowing experience with
pirates off the west coast of India. Ship captains regularly hired African
soldiers to protect them from pirate attacks. Ibn Battuta describes an
armed escort galley for merchant vessels.]

The infidels came out against us in twelve warships, fought fiercely
against us and overcame us. They took everything I had preserved for
emergencies; they took the pearls and rubies that the king of Ceylon
had given me, they took my clothes and the supplies given me by pious
people and saints. They left me no covering except my trousers. They
took everything everybody had and set us down on the shore. I returned
to Calicut and went into one of the mosques. One of the jurists sent me a
robe, and a qadi a turban and one of the merchants another robe. . . .

Qandahar is a large town belonging to the infidels and situated on
a tidal basin. The ships there lie on the mud at ebb-tide and float on
the water at high tide. The sultan of Qandahar is an infidel called Raja
Jalansi, who is under Muslim suzerainty [dominion] and sends a gift to
the king of India every year.

He came out to welcome us and showed us the greatest honour, himself leaving his palace and installing us in it. The principal Muslims at his
court came to visit us. One of these is the shipowner Ibrahim al-Jagir,
who possesses six vessels of his own.

We embarked on one of his ships. On this ship we put seventy of the
horses of Sultan Tughluq's presents [to the Chinese emperor], and the
rest we put with the horses of our companions on a ship belonging to
Ibrahim's brother.

Raja Jalansi gave us another vessel on which we put the horses of
Zahir ad-Din and Sunbul and the Chinese ambassador's party, and he
equipped it for us with water, provisions and forage. He sent his son
with us on a ship which resembled a galley, but is rather broader; it has

sixty oars and is covered with a roof during battle in order to protect the rowers from arrows and stones.

I myself went on board al-Jagir's ship, which had a complement of fifty rowers and fifty Abyssinian men-at-arms. These latter are the guarantors of safety on the Indian Ocean; let there be but one of them on a ship and it will be avoided by the Indian pirates and idolaters. . . .

[Following is one of several competing stories of how Islam arrived in the Maldives.]

It is a custom of theirs when a vessel arrives at their island that *kanadir*, that is to say small boats, go out to meet them, loaded with people from the island carrying betel and *karanbah*, that is, green coconuts. Each man of them gives these to anyone whom he chooses on board the vessel, and that person becomes his guest and carries his goods to his host's house as though he were one of his relatives. Any of the visitors who wish to marry may do so, but when it is time to leave he divorces the woman, because their women never leave the country. . . .

A number of trustworthy persons among the population such as the jurist Isa of al-Yaman, the jurist and teacher Ali, the qadi Abdallah, and others told me that these islanders were infidels and that every month there would appear to them an evil spirit, coming from the direction of the sea and resembling a ship filled with lights. On seeing him it was their custom to take a virgin girl and, after dressing her in finery, to conduct her to the *Budkhanah*, that is the idol-temple, which was built on the seashore and had a window looking out on the sea. There they would leave her for a night and when they came back in the morning they would find her violated and dead. So they went on drawing lots every month among themselves, and the one on whom the lot fell gave up his daughter. Then there came amongst them a man from the Maghrib [Maghreb, in northwestern Africa] called Abu'l Barakat al-Barbari, who could recite by heart the Holy Qur'an, and he lodged in the house of an old woman of their people in the island of Mahal. One day when he visited her, he found that she had called together all her kinswomen, and they were weeping as though they were at a funeral ceremony. He asked them what was the matter with them, but they did not explain it to him. Then an interpreter came and told him that the lot had fallen on the old woman, and she had but one daughter whom the evil spirit would kill. Abu'l Barakat said to her: "I shall go in place of your daughter tonight," for he was beardless, having no hair at all on his face. So they took him that night and brought him into the *Budkhanah*, he having previously made his ablutions, and he stayed there reciting the Qur'an. Then the evil spirit appeared to him from the window, but he continued his recitation and when the spirit came so near as to hear the recital, he plunged into the sea. In the morning the Maghribi was still occupied in his recitation when the old woman came with her kinsfolk and the people of the island to bring out the girl, as they had been accustomed to do, and burn her body. They found the Maghribi reciting, took him to their king who was called Shanuraza, and told the latter his story. The king was astonished at it and when the Maghribi expounded Islam to him and interested him in it he replied: "Stay with us until the next month; then if you repeat this action and escape the evil spirit I shall become a Muslim." So he stayed with them and Allah opened the breast of the king to Islam and he was converted before the end of the month, and his children and his court also.

When the next month opened the Maghribi was taken to the *Budkhanah*, but the demon did not come; he continued to recite the Qur'an till dawn, and when the sultan came along with the people and found him occupied in recitation they broke up the idols and destroyed the *Budkhanah*. The population of the island embraced Islam and sent word to all the other islands, whose populations were converted also. The Maghribi settled down among them, greatly venerated, and they adopted his rite, namely the rite of the Imam Malik, may God be pleased with him, and to this day they continue to hold the Maghribis in high respect because of him. He built a mosque which is known by his name. . . .

[Ibn Battuta stayed as a guest in the court of Sultan al-Malik al-Zahir in Samudera-Pasai, Indonesia. The city's rulers had been converted to Islam as a result of the work of Sufis who had been developing a presence in Southeast Asia over the course of two centuries. The tombstone of the first Islamic ruler in Samudera-Pasai, Sultan al-Malik al-Saleh, marks the beginning of Islam on the island.]

[We] reached the island of al-Jawa [Sumatra], from which *Jawi* incense takes its name. We saw it at a distance of half a day's sail. It is green and very well wooded with coconuts, areca palms, cloves, Indian aloes. . . . These people buy and sell with little pieces of tin or unrefined Chinese gold. Most of the aromatics there are in the part which belongs to the infidels; they are less common in the part belonging to the Muslims. When we reached the harbour its people came out to us in small boats with coconuts, bananas, mangoes, and fish. Their custom is to present these to the merchants, who recompense them, each according to his means. The admiral's representative also came on board, and after interviewing the merchants who were with us gave us permission to land. So we went ashore to the port, a large village on the coast with a number of houses, called Sarha. It is four miles distant from the town. The admiral's representative having written to the sultan to inform him of my arrival, the latter ordered the amir Dawlasa to meet me, along with the qadi and other doctors of the law. They came out for that purpose, bringing one of the sultan's horses and some other horses as well. I and my companions mounted, and we rode into the sultan's town, the capital of Sumatra, a large and beautiful city encompassed by a wooden wall with wooden towers.

The sultan of Java, al-Malik al-Zahir, is a most illustrious and openhanded ruler, and a lover of theologians. He is constantly engaged in warring for the Faith [against the infidels] and in raiding expeditions, but is withal a humble-hearted man, who walks on foot to the Friday prayers. His subjects also take pleasure in warring for the Faith and voluntarily accompany him on his expeditions. They have the upper hand over all the infidels in their vicinity, who pay them a poll-tax to keep the peace.

2

MARCO POLO

The Travels of Marco Polo

ca. 1294

Marco Polo was a thirteenth-century Venetian merchant whose travels took him to much of the Indian Ocean world. He left Europe for China in 1271. On his return to Venice, he traveled through parts of Southeast and South Asia. His accounts of his travels also include stories about East Africa, including the islands of Muslim-ruled Madagascar and Zanzibar. These accounts were recorded by the writer Rustichello da Pisa based on what Polo told him when they were both imprisoned in Genoa. Published

Marco Polo, *The Travels of Marco Polo*, trans. Henry Yule (New York: Sterling, 2012), 276, 282, 292, 297, 306–7, 312–15, 321.

in Old French as Livre des Merveilles du Monde *(Book of the Marvels of the World) at the turn of the fourteenth century, it was soon translated into Latin and Italian, among other languages. Polo's accounts were based on both firsthand information and hearsay.*

[In approximately 1294, Marco Polo stopped in Sumatra on his return journey from China. He refers to the island as "Java the Less" and notes Muslim merchants and the spread of Islam in Southeast Asia.]

When you leave the Island of Pentam and sail about 100 miles, you reach the Island of Java the Less. . . . Now I will tell you all about this Island.

You see there are upon it eight kingdoms and eight crowned kings. The people are all Idolaters, and every kingdom has a language of its own. The Island has a great abundance of treasure, with costly spices, lign-aloes [aromatic wood] and spikenard [perfumed ointment] and many others that never come into our parts.

Now I am going to tell you all about these eight kingdoms, or at least the greater part of them. But let me premise one marvelous thing, and that is the fact that this Island lies so far to the south that the North Star, little or much, is never to be seen!

. . . I will tell you of the kingdom of Ferlec. This kingdom, you must know, is so much frequented by the Saracen merchants that they have converted the natives to the Law of Muhammad—I mean the towns-people only, for the hill-people live for all the world like beasts, and eat human flesh, as well as all other kinds of flesh, clean or unclean. And they worship this, that, and the other thing; for in fact the first thing that they see on rising in the morning, that they do worship for the rest of the day.

[Here he describes the large imprint found in a rock near the summit of Sri Pada, known as Adam's Peak, a pilgrimage site in southern Sri Lanka. Muslims view it as the spot where Adam set foot after being exiled from Eden. Buddhists see it as Buddha's footprint; Hindus, as Lord Shiva's; and many Christians, as Saint Thomas's.]

The Idolaters come to that place on pilgrimage from very long distances and with great devotion. . . . But the Saracens also come there on pilgrimage in great numbers.

[Marco Polo describes what he saw in Gujarat (in western India).]

[Gujarat] is a great kingdom. The people are idolaters and have a peculiar language, and a king of their own, and are tributary to no one. . . . In this province of [Gujarat] there grows much pepper, and ginger, and indigo. They have also a great deal of cotton. Their cotton trees are of very great size, growing full six paces high, and attaining to an age of 20 years. . . . They dress in this country great numbers of skins of various kinds, goat-skins, ox-skins, buffalo and wild ox-skins. . . . In fact so many are dressed every year as to load a number of ships for Arabia and other quarters. They also work here beautiful mats in red and blue leather, exquisitely inlaid with figures of birds and beasts, and skillfully embroidered with gold and silver wire. These are marvellously beautiful things; they are used by the Saracens to sleep upon. . . .

[He heard the following things about Madagascar, Zanzibar, and Aden.]

Madagascar is an island towards the south, about a thousand miles from Socotra [east of the Horn of Africa and south of the Arabian Peninsula]. The people are all Saracens, adoring [Muhammad]. They have four *shayks*, or elders, who are said to govern the whole Island. And you must know that it is the most noble and beautiful Island, and one of the greatest in the world. . . . The people live by trade and handicrafts. . . . You must know that this Island lies so far south that ships cannot go further south or visit other Islands in that direction, except this one, and that other of which we have to tell you, called Zanghibar [Zanzibar]. This is because the sea-current runs so strong towards the south that the ships which should attempt it never would get back again. Indeed, the ships of Malabar [India] which visit this Island of [Madagascar], and that other of Zanghibar, arrive there with marvelous speed, for great as the distance is they accomplish it in 20 days, whilst the return voyage takes them more than 3 months. . . . Zanghibar is a great and noble Island. . . . The people are all Idolaters, and have a king and a language of their own. . . . The people live on rice and flesh and milk and dates; and they make wine of dates and of rice and of good spices and sugar. There is a great deal of trade. . . .

You must know that in the province of Aden there is a Prince who is called the [Sultan]. The people are all Saracens and adorers of [Muhammad]. . . . There are many towns and villages in the country.

This Aden is the port to which many of the ships of India come with their cargoes; and from this haven the merchants carry the goods a distance of seven days further in small vessels. At the end of those seven days they land the goods and load them on camels, and so carry them a land journey of 30 days. This brings them to the river of Alexandria, and by it they descend to the latter city. It is by this way through Aden that the Saracens of Alexandria receive all their stores of pepper and other spicery; and there is no other route equally good and convenient by which these goods could reach that place.

And you must know that the [Sultan] of Aden receives a large amount in duties from the ships that traffic between India and this country, importing different kinds of goods; and from the exports also he gets a revenue, for there are dispatched from the port of Aden to India a very large number of Arab chargers, and palfreys, and stout nags [types of horses] adapted for all work, which are a source of great profit to those who export them. For horses fetch very high prices in India, there being none bred there. . . . [The Sultan] of Aden receives heavy payments in port charges, so that it is said he is one of the richest princes in the world.

3

ZHENG HE

The Overall Survey of the Ocean's Shores
1433

During the early fifteenth century, the Ming dynasty emperor Yung-lo launched an ambitious plan to expand Chinese influence across the Indian Ocean. He commissioned nearly seventeen hundred new ships that would sail around the world, chart the oceans, and bring foreign polities within China's orbit. One of the emperor's confidants, Zheng He, who was of Arab-Mongol origin, was a Muslim whose father and grandfather had made the pilgrimage to Mecca. His knowledge of Arabic and Arab customs made him particularly suited to visit countries in which Islam was prominent or the state religion. Zheng He was made imperial envoy

Ma Huan, *Ying-yai Sheng-lan, The Overall Survey of the Ocean's Shores [1433]*, trans. J. V. G. Mills (Cambridge: Cambridge University Press, 1970), 47–50, 69–70.

and admiral of the Ming fleet and prepared the first expedition into the Western Ocean in 1405. Over the next twenty-eight years, he led seven expeditions, visiting dozens of countries from Southeast Asia to East Africa. Ma Huan, the Muslim Chinese translator who accompanied him on his last four voyages, wrote The Overall Survey of the Ocean's Shores *in 1433.*

Southeast Asia

Aru [Deli, in northern Sumatra]. Ships reached here after a voyage of four days from Malacca. On the north lay the great sea, on the south great mountains, on the east flat land, and on the west the country of Semudera [Samudera-Pasai, in northern Sumatra]. The people practiced agriculture and fishing. Customs were identical with those of Java and Malacca. Islam prevailed. Products included lign-aloes and benzoin [a type of resin used for perfumes].

Semudera. This formed the principal emporium for the Western Ocean. From Malacca ships steered towards the south-west, and they arrived here after five days' sailing. The great sea formed the northern boundary, on the south and east rose great mountains, and the great sea lay away to the west. A pretender named Sekandar, rebelling against the reigning king, was captured by Zheng He [on his fourth expedition] and taken to China; the king, in gratitude, constantly sent tribute to the Chinese court. People cultivated dry-land rice. . . . Pepper from local gardens [was] sold. . . . Cattle-breeding was extensively practiced. Language, writing, and marriage and funeral customs coincided with those of Malacca. . . .

Lambri [Aceh, in northern Sumatra]. Ships reached here after sailing due west from Semudera for three days. The great sea was on the north and west [and] mountains on the south. . . . The king held the Muslim faith. Traders used copper coins. Products included laka-wood [a dark-colored wood] and rhinoceros. . . . The king of Lambri constantly sent tribute to China. . . .

South Asia

Cochin [Kochi, in southwest India]. This country, one day's sailing north-west from Quilon [Kollam, in southwest India], lay beside the sea, had large mountains on the east, and was linked by road with neighboring countries. King and people belonged to the Chola race. The population consisted of five kinds of persons; first, the honourable Nan-k'un

[Brahmin or Kshatriya]; secondly, Muslims; thirdly, the moneyed Che-ti [Chetty]; fourthly, the Ko-ling [Kling] brokers; and fifthly, the untouchable Mu-kua [Mukava]. The king devoutly worshipped Buddha. A class of religious devotees bore the appellation Cho-chi [Jogi]. Pepper, the only product, was extensively cultivated, and was bought and stored by local merchants until foreigners came to buy it, the price being ninety gold coins, worth five Chinese "ounces" of silver. . . . The Chetties dealt in gems, pearls, aromatics, and corals. The king minted a gold *fanam* and a silver *tar*, worth one-fifteenth of a *fanam*. In marriages and funerals the five kinds of persons followed their own customs. The king sent tribute to China.

Calicut [Kozhikode, in southwest India]. This constituted the great country of the Western Ocean, being three days' sailing north-west from Cochin. On the north lay Honavar, on the south Cochin, on the west the great sea, and on the east men travelled through the mountains to Coimbatore. Zheng He [on his second expedition] visited the king, and erected a commemorative plaque. The king was a Nan-k'un man, and a devout Buddhist. The population included the same five kinds of persons as in Cochin.

The king and the people refrained from eating beef, while the great chiefs, being Muslims, refrained from eating pork. The king built a temple of Buddha, cast a brass image of Buddha and washed it daily. Watered ox-dung was smeared over the ground and walls of the temple, and over the person of the king and chiefs. Two Muslim chiefs administered the country. The majority of the people professed the Muslim religion, and once in seven days they worshipped in twenty or thirty temples. On the visits of the Chinese treasure-ships, Indian and Chinese officials fixed the exchange-values of the Chinese silks and other goods, and the values were reduced to writing and strictly adhered to when the local traders exchanged their gems and other valuables. The Indians, using no apparatus but the digits of hands and feet, made unerring calculations. . . . Customs differed according as the people were Cholas or Muslims. The royal succession ran through the son of the king's sister. . . .

Maldive and Laccadive islands. From Poulo Weh ships steered southwest, and could reach the islands in ten days. . . . King, chiefs, and people professed the Muslim religion. The people lived by fishing and cultivating coconuts. In their marriage- and funeral-rites they followed the tenets of their religion. Coconuts abounded and were exported to foreign countries. In ship-construction they fastened planks with cords and used no nails. Ambergris sold for its weight in silver. They exported cowries and dried bonito fish for sale abroad. They manufactured superior silk kerchiefs. The king minted a small silver coin. One or two Chinese treasure-ships visited the islands. . . .

Bengal. Ships travelled from Semudera . . . and made Chittagong after twenty days. . . . The country was extensive, productive, and well-populated. Numerous wealthy ship-owners traded overseas, and many labourers sought employment abroad. The people were all Muslims, speaking Bengali and occasionally Persian. The king minted a silver *tanka,* and cowries might also be used as currency. Popular customs conformed with religion. They had public baths and all kinds of shops. They manufactured half a dozen kinds of fine cloths, besides the silks and many miscellaneous articles, including fine steel. Punishments included flogging and banishment. They had a service of administrative and military officials, also doctors, astrologers, and experts of all kinds. The king carried on foreign trade, and he presented valuable tribute to China. . . .

Arabia and Persian Gulf

Dhufar [Dhofar, in southern Oman]. Ships leaving Calicut steered northwest and arrived after ten days. The country lay between the sea on the south-east and mountains on the north-west. King and people held the Muslim faith. Mounted soldiers and a military band accompanied the king when he travelled. On the day of worship the men stopped trading before noon, bathed and perfumed themselves, and went to worship in the mosques. Marriage- and funeral-rites were prescribed by religion. The land produced frankincense, and when the Chinese treasure-ships visited the place, the people traded frankincense and other articles for silks and porcelain. The Chinese found ostriches and camels there. The king minted a gold *tanka* and a copper coin. The king sent frankincense, ostriches, and other such things as tribute to China.

Aden [in southern Yemen]. From Calicut the junks steered due west and reached Aden after one month. In this rich and populous sea-side country king and people were Muslims, and spoke Arabic. The country had a powerful and menacing army. On Zheng He's [sixth] expedition of 1421 the fleet was divided at Semudera, and the eunuch Chou reached Aden with several treasure-ships; the king extended an enthusiastic and elaborate welcome to the Chinese mission; and [they] purchased many rare articles, animals, and birds. The jewelers manufactured *objets d'art* of unequalled beauty. Aden had markets, public baths, and shops selling goods of every kind. The king minted a gold *fuluri* and a copper *fulus.* Astrologers made accurate prognostications of the seasons, eclipses, tides, and weather. Among unusual animals seen there were the big-tailed sheep, zebra, ostrich, giraffe, and lion. The king sent valuable gifts as tribute to China. . . .

Hormuz [in southern Iran]. Ships leaving Calicut steered north-west and arrived at Hormuz after twenty-five days. Foreign trade enriched the population. King and people zealously performed their religious duties as Muslims. Marriage- and funeral-rites conformed with Islam. The king minted a silver *dinar*. They wrote in "Muslim" [Arabic] characters. Civil and military officials, doctors, and craftsmen excelled. Minerals were quarried under official supervision. Imported cereals were cheap. Goods, including imported luxuries, abounded. Unusual animals included the lynx.

Mecca. From Calicut ships steered south-west, and after three months made Jeddah, whence Mecca could be reached in a day. Here was founded the Muslim religion, which all the inhabitants professed and devoutly followed. They spoke the Arabic language. They formed a law-abiding and happy community. Marriage- and funeral-rites were ordained by their religion. Within the great mosque stood the perfumed Heavenly Hall, the "K'ai-a-pai" [Ka'ba]. . . . Foreign Muslims came annually to worship, each pilgrim removing a portion of the silk covering as a memento. Near the Ka'ba lay the tomb of Isma'il, a holy man. From the four towers of the mosque the call to prayer was made, and the service chanted. The king minted a very pure gold *tanka*. In Medina lay the tomb of the holy Muhammad. . . . The king of Mecca sent tribute to the Chinese court.

2

Trade, Society, and Social Customs

By the late twelfth century, Muslims had gained a foothold in ports across the region, from Kilwa in East Africa to Sumatra in Southeast Asia. Often complementing the observations made by Ibn Battuta, Marco Polo, and Zheng He, the following documents highlight various aspects of Islam in the Indian Ocean world, including the role of Muslim merchants in spreading Islam through trade, the range of social customs in the various regions, and the different kinds of societies into which Islam was assimilated and that Islam helped transform.

4

ABD-ER-RAZZAK

Narrative of the Journey of Abd-er-Razzak
1442

The narrative of the fifteenth-century ambassador of Shah Rukh, ruler of the Timurid dynasty in Persia, to the court of Calicut, India, is based on his journey between 1442 and 1445. It is part of a much larger work titled Matla' us-Sa'dain wa Majma' ul-Bahrain *(The Rising of the Auspicious Twin-Stars, and the Confluence of the Ocean). Here he details the extraordinary range of merchants who circulated around the Indian Ocean trade networks. He also points to the distinctions between Muslim and non-Muslim locals in India, elaborating on the matrilineal system of inheritance, the caste system, and the variety of cultures and traditions.*

"Narrative of the Journey of Abd-er-Razzak, Ambassador from Shah Rukh, A.H. 845, A.D. 1442," in *India in the Fifteenth Century: Being a Collection of Narrative Voyages to India*, ed. R. H. Major (London: Hakluyt Society, 1857), 3–17.

Narrative of my voyage into Hindoostan, and description of the wonder of Remarkable Peculiarities which this country presents.

Every man, the eyes of whose intelligence are illuminated by the light of truth, and whose soul, like a bird, soars with fixedness of vision into the regions of knowledge, observes with certainty, and brings home to his recognition the fact that the revolution of the great bodies which people the heavens, as well as the progress of the smaller bodies which canopy the earth, are subject to the wisdom and the will of a Creator, Who is alike holy and powerful . . . [so] that the proudest existences are forced to bow the head beneath the commands of Allah. . . .

The events, the perils which accompany a voyage by sea (and which in themselves constitute a shoreless and boundless ocean), present the most marked indication of the Divine omnipotence, the grandest evidence of a wisdom which is sublime. . . .

In pursuance of the orders of Providence, and of the decrees of that Divine prescience, the comprehension of which escapes all the calculations and reflections of man, I received orders to take my departure for India. . . .

Continuing my journey, I arrived . . . at the shore of the Sea of Oman, and at Bender-Ormuz. The prince of Ormuz, Melik-Fakhr-Eddin-Touranschah, having placed a vessel at my disposal, I went on board of it, and made my entry, with everything that I could require, and I was admitted to audience of the prince.

Ormuz . . . is a port situated in the middle of the sea, and which has not its equal on the surface of the globe. The merchants of seven climates from Egypt, Syria, the country of Roum [the Arabic name for Anatolia], [Azerbaijan], Irak-Arabi, and Irak-Adjemi . . . the whole of the kingdoms of Tchin [China], and Matchin [southern parts of China], and the city of Khanbalik [former name of Beijing], all make their way to this port; the inhabitants of the sea coasts arrive here from the countries of Tchin, Java, Bengal, the cities of Zirbad ["the country under the wind," referencing the southeastern part of India] . . . [Socotra] . . . the islands of Diwah-Mahall [the Maldives], the countries of Malabar, Abyssinia, Zaguebar, the ports of . . . [Gujarat], [Cambay], the coasts of Arabia, which extend as far as Aden, [Jeddah], and Yanbu; they bring those rare and precious articles which the sun, the moon, and the rains have combined to bring to perfection, and which are capable of being transported by sea. Travellers from all countries resort here, and, in exchange for commodities which they bring, they can without trouble or difficulty, obtain all that they desire. Bargains are made either by money or exchange. For all objects, with the exception of gold and silver, a tenth of their value is paid by way of duty.

Persons of all religions, and even idolaters, are found in great numbers in this city, and no injustice is permitted toward any person whatever. This city is also named Dar-alaman (the abode of security). . . .

I sojourned in this place for the space of two months . . . so that the favorable time for departing by sea, that is to say the beginning or middle of the monsoon, was allowed to pass, and we came to the end of the monsoon, which is the season when tempests and attacks from pirates are to be dreaded. Then they gave me permission to depart. As the men and horses could not all be contained in the same vessel, they were distributed among several ships. The sails were hoisted, and we commenced our voyage.

[After] some difficulties [we] disembarked at the port of Muscat. For myself, I quitted this city, escorted by the principal companions of my voyage, and went to a place called Kairat, where I established myself and fixed my tents, with the intention of there remaining. . . . In consequence of the severity of pitiless weather and the adverse manifestations of a treacherous fate, my heart was crushed like glass and my soul became weary of life, and my season of relaxation became excessively trying to me. . . .

Calicut is a perfectly secure harbor, which, like that of Ormuz, brings together merchants from every city and from every country; in it are to be found abundance of precious articles brought there from maritime countries, and especially from Abyssinia, Zirbad, and Zangueba; from time to time ships arrive there from shores of the House of Allah [Mecca] and other parts of the [Hijaz], and abide at will, for a greater or longer space, in this harbor; the town is inhabited by Infidels, and situated on a hostile shore. It contains a considerable number of Muslims, who are constant residents, and have built two mosques, in which they meet every Friday to offer up prayer. They have one Kadi, a priest[,] and for the most part they belong to the sect of Schafei [Shafi'i]. Security and justice are so firmly established in this city, that the wealthiest merchants bring to this place from maritime countries considerable cargoes, which they unload, and unhesitatingly send into the markets and the bazaars. . . . When a sale is made, they levy a duty on the goods of one-fortieth part; if they are not sold they make no charge on them whatsoever.

[At] Calicut, every ship, whatever place it may come from, or wherever it may be bound, when it puts in to this port is treated like other vessels, and has no trouble of any kind to put up with. . . .

The sound of [the] Khutba[1] [has] become so acceptable to the world, that all the infidels have shown themselves willing to adopt it.

---

[1] A sermon preached every Friday after the service in the principal mosque.

[Deputies], setting out in company with the ambassadors from Bengal, reached the noble court of the emperor, and the Emirs laid before that monarch the letter and the presents by which it was accompanied. The messenger was a [Muslim], distinguished for his eloquence; in the course of his address he said to the prince, "If your majesty will be pleased to favor my master, by dispatching an ambassador sent especially to him, and who, in literal pursuance of the precept expressed in that verse, 'By your wisdom by your good counsels engage men to enter in the ways of your Lord,' shall invite that prince to embrace the religion of Islamism, and draw from his beclouded heart the bolt of Islamism, and draw from his beclouded heart the bolt of darkness and error, and cause the flame of the light of faith, and the brightness of the sun of knowledge to shine into the window of his heart, it will be, beyond all doubt, a perfectly righteous and meritorious deed." The emperor acceded to this request, and gave instructions to the Emirs that the ambassador should make his preparations for setting out on his journey. . . .

As to the [Muslims in Calicut], they dress themselves in magnificent apparel after the manner of the Arabs, and manifest luxury in every particular. After I had had an opportunity of seeing a considerable number of [Muslims] and Infidels, I had a comfortable lodging assigned to me, and after the lapse of three days was conducted to an audience with the king. I saw a man with his body naked, like the rest of the Hindus. The sovereign of this city bears the title of Sameri. When he dies it is his sister's son who succeeds him, and his inheritance does not belong to his son or his brother, or any other of his relations. No one reaches the throne by means of the strong hand.

The Infidels are divided into a great number of classes, such as the [Brahmins], the Djohis [Hindu ascetics], and others. Although they are all agreed upon the fundamental principles of polytheism and idolatry, each sect has its peculiar customs. Among them there is a class of men, with whom it is the practice for one woman to have a great number of husbands, each of whom undertakes a special duty and fulfils it. The hours of the day and of the night are divided between them; each of them for a certain period takes up his abode in the house, and while he remains there no other is allowed to enter. The Sameri belongs to this sect.

5

MUHAMMAD IBN ASAD JALAL UD-DIN AL-DAWWANI

Jalalean Ethics

ca. 1475

The following fifteenth-century Persian work by Muhammad Ibn Asad Jalal ud-din al-Dawwani provides the economic justification for distinct classes within a society, of which enslaved subjects were also a critical part. The work was popular in Mughal India, where, as elsewhere in the Indian Ocean world, slaves were bought from abroad and sold to supplement existing labor. Theese slaves performed many functions, including as soldiers, palace guards, eunuch guards in harems, craftsmen, construction workers, administrators, teachers, domestic servants, wet-nurses, and concubines. Akhlaq-i-Jalali (Jalali's Ethics) delineates four classes within society. Although the divisions are gendered male, women were nevertheless parts of the various divisions and subdivisions.

In order to preserve this political equipoise, there is a correspondence to be maintained between the various classes. Like as the equipoise of bodily temperament is affected by intermixture and correspondence of four elements, the equipoise of the political temperament is to be sought for in the correspondence of four classes.

1. *Men of the pen*, such as lawyers, divines, judges, bookmen, statisticians, geometricians, astronomers, physicians, poets. In these and their exertions in the use of their delightful pens, the subsistence of the faith and of the world itself is vested and bound up. They occupy the place in politics that water does among the elements. Indeed, to persons of ready understanding, the similarity of knowledge and water is as clear as water itself, and as evident as the sun that makes it so.

2. *Men of the sword*, such as soldiers, fighting zealots, guards of forts and passes, etc.; without whose exercise of the impetuous and vindictive

Muhammad Ibn Asad Jalal ud-din al-Dawwani, *Jalalean Ethics*, trans. W. F. Thompson in *The Practical Philosophy of the Muhammadan People* (London: Oriental Translation Fund, 1839), 388–90, in *Sources of Indian Tradition*, vol. 1, *From the Beginning to 1800*, ed. Ainslie T. Embree (New York: Columbia University Press, 1988), 431.

sword, no arrangement of the age's interests could be effected; without the havoc of whose tempest-like energies, the materials of corruption, in the shape of rebellious and disaffected persons, could never be dissolved and dissipated. These then occupy the place of fire, their resemblance to it is too plain to require demonstration; no rational person need call in the aid of fire to discover it.

3. *Men of business*, such as merchants, capitalists, artisans, and craftsmen, by whom the means of emolument and all other interests are adjusted; and through whom the remotest extremes enjoy the advantage and safeguard of each other's most peculiar commodities. The resemblance of these to air—the auxiliary of growth and increase in vegetables—the reviver of spirit in animal life—the medium by the undulation and movement of which all sorts of rare and precious things traverse the hearing to arrive at the headquarters of human nature—is exceedingly manifest.

4. *Husbandmen*, such as seedsmen, bailiffs, and agriculturists—the superintendents of vegetation and preparers of provender; without whose exertions the continuance of the human kind must be cut short. These are, in fact, the only producers of what had no previous existence; the other classes adding nothing whatever to subsisting products, but only transferring what subsists already from person to person, from place to place, and from form to form. How close these come to the soil and surface of the earth—the point to which all the heavenly circles refer—the scope to which all the luminaries of the purer world direct their rays—the stage on which wonders are displayed—the limit to which mysteries are confined—must be universally apparent.

In like manner then as in the composite organizations the passing of any element beyond its proper measure occasions the loss of equipoise, and is followed by dissolution and ruin, in political coalition, no less, the prevalence of any one class over the other three overturns the adjustment and dissolves the junction.

6

AHMAD IBN MAJID

Two Selections on Navigation

The most detailed account of the Indian Ocean itself—its various seas, coasts, gulfs, and straits—comes from the fifteenth-century Omani navigator and cartographer Ahmad Ibn Majid. The author of several works, he wrote Kitab al-Fawa'id fi Usul 'Ilm al-Bahr wa l'-Qawa'id *(Book of Useful Information on the Rules of Navigation) in 1490. It is somewhat analogous to the anonymously written Alexandrian Greek travel guide* Periplus of the Erythraean Sea, *from over a millennium earlier, or the* Chu-fan shi, *by the thirteenth-century Chinese author Chau Ju-kua, in that it is a technical guide for seafarers interspersed with various personal observations. According to secondary accounts, Ibn Majid is said to have guided Vasco da Gama across the Indian Ocean from Malindi to Calicut in 1498, although this has been disputed by historians. Like all Muslim authors, Ibn Majid begins his* Kitab *with the* bismillah *(the Arabic phrase "In the name of Allah"). In the first selection, Ibn Majid emphasizes the religious importance in determining one's bearings at sea—that is, to know which way to face for prayer, called the* qibla, *or the direction toward Mecca. In the second selection,* Gathering of the Summarizing of the Concerning the First Principles of the Knowledge of the Seas, *written in 1492, Ibn Majid expresses his concerns over intermarriage between Muslims and non-Muslims.*

Book of Useful Information on the Rules of Navigation

1490

In the name of God, the Merciful, the Compassionate. Praise be to God and prayer and peace be upon the best of his lieutenants, Muhammad, and on his family and Companions.

G. R. Tibbetts, *Arab Navigation in the Indian Ocean before the Portuguese* (London: Royal Asiatic Society of Great Britain and Ireland, 1971), 65–66, 194–95.

Verily I have seen sciences in this world more worthy of glory, more exalted in rank and more meritorious, for did not the Prophet say, "All the other Prophets enjoined people to seek after knowledge."[1] . . .

[Travel by sea was perilous not only because of shifting weather patterns and the possibility of pirate attacks, but also because animosities could grow aboard ship, both among the crew members and between the crew members and passengers. Ibn Majid offers advice to captains on how to maintain order and travel as safely as possible.]

If a man wishes to do anything [by methods] not connected with the science of navigation, then he can do so, but whenever he lacks the Qibla directions of towns and islands which are in the Encircling Ocean, then he must find them by means of our science. So strive after it and knowledge will come bit by bit, for the learning of it can only come to an end at the end of one's life and he who never overtakes anything will never leave it behind. . . .

Be full of prayers to prevent misfortunes and sometimes misfortune comes to you which is not your own fault. . . . It was said to a man, "How do you recognize your Lord," and he replied, "When the will to resist fades away." So beware whenever your enemy faces you in your ship, for he will only face you in order to corrupt your affair aiming to make you do evil things. But the wise man will be quick to deal with him. Be quick to make a decision. Be silent or give answers the consequence of which will not harm you and do not commit you to anything. It is necessary when you sail to be clean. And when you are on the ship you are one of the creator's guests so do not neglect to mention him.

. . . Forbid those who sail from making fun of others on the sea; it will only result in evil, hatred and enmity and he who does this continually will not be spared from grudge or hatred or contempt. . . . [Finally,] consult other people and improve your own opinion.

---

[1]The Arabic word *'ilm* can be translated as both "knowledge" and "science." This quotation cannot be identified in the Hadith.

*Gathering of the Summarizing of the Concerning the First
Principles of the Knowledge of the Seas*
1462

The harbour of Malacca is between Pulau Ubi and Sabta. So enter the port successfully moving through five fathoms to four then anchor. The people then come out to you—and what people. They have no culture at all. The infidel marries Muslim women while the Muslim takes pagans to wife. You do not know whether they are Muslim or not. They are thieves for theft is rife among them and they do not mind. The Muslim eats dogs for meat for there are no food laws. They drink wine in the markets and do not treat divorce as a religious act.

Shihab al-Din Ahmad Ibn Majid, in *Hawiyat al-Ikhtisar fi 'Ilm al-Bihar* (*Gathering of the Summarizing of the Concerning the First Principles of the Knowledge of the Seas*), MS. 2292, "Al-Mal'aqiya," in *A Study of the Arabic Texts Containing Material of South-East Asia*, trans. G. R. Tibbetts (Leiden: Brill, 1979), 205–6.

7

ZAIN AL-DIN AL-MALIBARI

Gift of the Mujahidin
1583

Zain al-Din al-Malibari was a sixteenth-century Malabar Muslim of Yemeni origin. These are excerpts from his Tuhfat al-Mujahidin *(Gift of the Mujahidin), which breaks down the often sharp and inaccurate distinctions made between Muslims and non-Muslims in the Indian Ocean world. The cross-cultural interactions that emerge from his account show*

Zain al-Din, *Tuhfat al-Mujahidin fi-ba'd akhbar al-Burtughaliyyin*, ed. Hamza Chelakodan (Calicut: Maktabat al-Huda, 1996), in *Islam in South Asia in Practice*, ed. Barbara D. Metcalf (Princeton, N.J.: Princeton University Press, 2009), 404–8.

*how Muslims gradually became a vital part of this region of India, albeit
always as a minority. Al-Malibari's ability to convey multiple perspectives
reflects his being both an insider and an outsider in relation to Malabar
society.*

In the Name of Allah, the Merciful, the Compassionate. . . .

Know that among the infidels of Malabar are strange customs unknown
in other regions. Among these is that if their leader is killed in battle, his
soldiers will fall upon his adversary and his adversary's town until they
themselves are all killed; or they destroy the whole kingdom of his adversary. Because of this Malabaris greatly dread killing leaders. This is an
old custom, even if they hold less to it in this age.

Among these customs is that the people of Malabar are of two divisions:
those allied with the Samuri [king of Calicut] and those allied with the
leader of Cochin. This division remains unless an attack or disturbance
occurs, and when that disappears, they return to their initial division.

Among these customs is that they do not employ deception in warfare. They designate a known day for the hostilities, and do not deviate
from it. They view treachery in this matter a disgrace. . . .

Of these customs is that among the Nayar and those related to them,
inheritance goes to the mother's brothers, or to the children of their sisters or their mothers' sisters or relatives on the mother's side. The children inherit neither money nor property. This custom—I mean the non-
inheritance of the children—has spread to the Muslims of Cannanore
and their followers nearby, even though among them are those who read
and memorize the Qur'an, who read it well, are knowledgeable in religion and are active in the rituals of worship. . . .

Among their customs is that two or four or more men agree upon one
woman of the Nayar group or those close to them, each one spending a
night with her in turn, just as the Muslim husband is divided among his
wives. Little enmity or rancor arises among them in this. The carpenters,
the ironsmiths, the gold and silversmiths, and the like, follow the Brahmins in having more than one man agreeing upon one woman, except
that here the men are brothers or relatives in order that the inheritance
not be fragmented, and in order to minimize disputes over inheritance. . . .

And among these customs is that they are subject to many burdensome ceremonies which they do not deviate from, because they are
divided into many sorts: among them the highest and the lowest, and
those in between. If contact occurs between the highest and the lowest,

or in a similar way proximity to a known degree between them and one of the lowly agriculturalists, the higher status one has to undergo a ritual washing. They do not permit him to eat food before washing. If he does eat before washing, he is demoted and no longer included with them in their high station. There is no salvation for him but in fleeing to a place where no one knows his circumstances. Otherwise, the chief of the town takes him and sells him to one below him in rank, in the event that he is a youth or a woman. Or else he comes to us and converts to Islam, or becomes a Yogi [Hindu] or a Christian. In this way, they do not permit the superior to consume food cooked by the inferior, for eating outside of his rank entails the above-mentioned consequences.

The people of the thread, i.e., those who are required to wear the string across their shoulders, are the most eminent of all the unbelievers of Malabar. And among them are subdivisions: the highest, the lowest, and those in between. The Brahmins are the highest of the people of the thread, and they are composed of classes. Apart from the people of the thread, there are the Nayar: they are the soldiers of the people of Malabar, and the mightiest and most numerous of them. They are also composed of different classes, the highest and the lowest among them, and those in between. Apart from these are the coconut pickers. They are the ones who climb the coconut trees in order to throw their coconuts down to the ground to extract their water, which becomes an intoxicant or is cooked and made into sugar.

And apart from them are the carpenters, and the ironsmiths, and the gold and silversmiths, and the fishermen, and others. There are yet others, the lowliest—who are involved in ploughing and planting, and related activities; they are also composed of different sorts. And if a pebble is cast by one of the low-status males at a woman of higher status on one of the nights of the year known among them, she is dropped from her station if she is not accompanied by a male, even if she is pregnant. The governor will either take and sell her, or bring her to us whereupon she converts to Islam; or she becomes a Christian or a Yogi. . . .

How many are the burdensome customs they impose upon themselves, in their ignorance and their foolishness. Allah most high and praised has made this the principal reason for their entry into the religion of Islam, by His bounty.

This talk however is a digression, for words lead to more words. Let us return to our purpose in these pages. Thus when Sharaf bin Malik—and Malik bin Dinar, and Habib bin Malik, and others mentioned earlier—entered Malabar and built mosques in the aforementioned port towns and spread in them the religion of Islam, its folk entered Islam little by little. And merchants came to Malabar from many regions, and they built up other towns, such as Calicut, Veliyankode, and Tirurangadi. . . . Their populations increased and prospered with Muslims and their commerce, on account of the little injustice found among their chiefs, even though they and their soldiers were unbelievers, and even though their subjects hold to their aforementioned customs and rarely transgress them. The Muslims in Malabar were subjects, small in number—not exceeding one-tenth of the society.

The greatest of the Malabar ports from ancient times and the most famous of them by reputation was the port of Calicut. But it became weak and fell into disrepair after the Portuguese arrived and disrupted the travels of its people. In all of the Malabar lands, the Muslims had no mighty prince ruling over them. Their rulers were unbelievers who governed them by supervising their affairs and by imposing fines upon those who deserved them under prevailing custom. Nonetheless, the Muslims enjoyed respect and standing, because most of the buildings in the towns were theirs, and they were able to hold Friday congregational prayers and festivals. They appointed judges and mu'azzins for the call to prayer, and carried out Islamic law among the Muslims. They did not permit disruption of the Friday prayers, and anyone who did so was accosted and fined in most towns. And if a Muslim commits a crime deserving among them of execution, they execute him with the permission of the leading Muslims. Then the Muslims take him and wash and prepare him, say the funeral prayer for him, and bury him in the Muslim cemetery. And if an unbeliever commits a crime deserving of execution, they kill him, crucify him, and leave him where he was slain, until the dogs and the jackals eat him.

They do not take other than the one-tenth tax on trade, except for fines, if actions are committed which among them require penalty. And they do not take land taxes from the farmers and gardeners, even if they be many. They do not enter the houses of the Muslims without their permission if a Muslim commits a crime, even if it be an unjust murder. Rather, they get the Muslims themselves to eject him from the house by perseverance, starvation, or like methods. They do not subject to harm anyone of them who converts to Islam; instead, they respect him as they do other Muslims, even if he is from one of their lowliest groups. The Muslim traders in the olden days took up collections for the convert.

8

TOMÉ PIRES

Suma Oriental

1512–1515

The sixteenth-century Portuguese observer Tomé Pires served Prince Afonso, son of King John II of Portugal. In 1511, Pires traveled to India as "factor of drugs" (that is, selling medicines) and was subsequently transferred to Malacca in Malaysia. He wrote most of his Suma Oriental *while living there over a three-year period. He concluded his career as Portugal's ambassador to China, where he lived for twenty years. His descriptions of trade from Malaysia westward across the Indian Ocean offer additional insight into Muslim practices in the region. Like Ibn Battuta's accounts (Document 1), Pires's are notable for their detail. Here he praises Gujarati merchants, urging Portuguese merchants to learn from them how to conduct business.*

Arabia Felix (southern Arabia)

The people of this Arabia are clean and noble. They have fortresses and horsemen. They are at war with Abyssinia, which borders on this Arabia, and they make raids on horseback, in the course of which they capture large numbers of Abyssinians whom they sell to the people of Asia. This land has wheat and good water. People come to trade in these ports from many places, from Cambay; from Aden. They bring coarse cloths of many kinds, glass beads, and other beads from Cambay; from Aden they bring raisins, from Ormuz dates, and they take back gold, ivory, and slaves and trade with them in the said ports of Zeila and Berbera [on the Horn of Africa, facing the Gulf of Aden]. They trade with other places too. Goods are brought from Kilwa, Malindi, Brava, Mogadishu, and [Mombasa] in exchange for the good horses in this Arabia. They

Tomé Pires, *Suma Oriental of Tomé Pires: An Account of the East, from the Red Sea to China, Written in Malacca and India in 1512–1515*, ed. Armando Cortesão (London: Hakluyt Society, 1944), 14, 41–43, 46–47.

have no cities and no king. They live in bands. They are a plundering people and very wild. These two ports are an outlet for the whole [of] Abyssinia. . . .

How They Trade in General: Cairo

The merchants from Cairo bring the merchandise which comes from Italy and Greece and Damascus to Aden, such as gold, silver, . . . vermilion, copper, rosewater, . . . colored woolen cloth, glass beads, weapons and things of that kind.

[The merchants of] Aden bring the above-mentioned goods with the addition of . . . raisins, opium, rosewater, quantities of gold and silver, and horses that Aden gets from Zeila and Berbera and the islands of [Sawakin], in the Strait, and from Arabia, and they come to do business in Cambay. They take back with them all the products of Malacca: cloves, nutmeg, mace, sandalwood, brazil woods, silks, seed pearls, musk, porcelain, and other things which may be [in the list of] merchandise from Malacca, as well as the following from the country itself: rice, wheat, soap, indigo, butter (and lard), oils, . . . coarse pottery like that from Seville, and all kinds of cloth, for trading in [Zeila], Berbera, [Socotra], Kilwa, Malindi, Mogadishu, and other places in Arabia. And this trade is carried out by ships from Aden and ships from Cambay, many of one and many of the other. . . .

On Gujarati Traders

They are men who understand merchandise; they are so properly steeped in the sound and harmony of it, that the Gujartis say that any offense connected with merchandise is pardonable. . . . Those of our people who want to be clerks or factors ought to go [to Gujarat] and learn, because the business of trade is a science in itself which does not hinder any other noble exercise, but helps a great deal. . . .

The Merchants Who Come and Start Companies (in Cambay) for Malacca

As the kingdom of Cambay had this trade with Malacca, merchants of the following nations used to accompany the Gujaratis there in their ships, and some of them used to settle in the place, sending off the merchandise, while others took it in person, to wit, Macaris and people from

Cairo, many Arabs, chiefly from Aden, and with these came Abyssinians, and people from Ormuz, Kilwa, Malindi, Mogadishu, and [Mombasa], Persians to wit, . . . Turkomans, Armenians, . . . Khorasans, and men of Shiraz. There are many of these in Malacca; and many people from the kingdom of the Deccan used to take up their companies in Cambay. The trade of Cambay is extensive and comprises cloths of many kinds and of a fair quality, rough clothing, seeds such as nigella, cumin, . . . and other things of the kind. They return loaded up [with] all the rich merchandise of the Moluccas, Banda, and China, and they used to bring a great deal of gold.

9

DUARTE BARBOSA

The Book of Duarte Barbosa

ca. 1516

Duarte Barbosa, an early-sixteenth-century Portuguese officer in India and author of Livro de Duarte Barbosa *(The Book of Duarte Barbosa), served as a scribe at the Portuguese factory (trading station) in Cannanore, on the west coast of India. In his book, he discusses the complex relay trades among Muslim merchants that linked small production and exchange locations with large port cities. Approximately three years after completing the book, he set off to circumnavigate the globe but died in the Philippines in 1521.*

[The Muslims] are great barterers, and deal in cloth, gold, ivory, and [diverse] other wares with the Moors [Muslims] and Heathen of the great kingdom of Cambaya; and to their haven come every year many ships with cargoes [of] merchandise, from which they get great store of gold, ivory and wax. In this traffic, the Cambaya merchants make great profits and thus, on one side and the other, they earn much money.

Duarte Barbosa, *The Book of Duarte Barbosa: An Account of the Countries Bordering on the Indian Ocean and Their Inhabitants*, 2 vols. (London: Hakluyt Society, 1918, 1921), 1:6–8, 22–23; 2:74–78.

There is great plenty of food in this city, rice, millet, and some wheat which they bring from Cambaya.

[Barbosa also provides a description of the major long-distance trade routes from Malabar to the Red Sea. At Calicut he wrote the following:]

[The Muslim traders] took on board goods for every place, and every monsoon ten and fifteen of these ships sailed for [the] Red Sea, Aden and Mecca, where they sold their goods at a profit, some . . . would go to Cairo, and from Cairo to Alexandria and then to Venice, where they came to our regions. These goods were pepper (great store), ginger, cinnamon, cardamons, . . . precious stones of every kind, seed pearls, musk, [a] great store of cotton cloths, porcelains, and some of them took on . . . many other things which they brought back for sale in Calecut. They started in February, and returned from the middle of August up to the middle of October of the same year. In this trade they became extremely wealthy. And on their return voyages they would bring with them other foreign merchants who settled in the city, beginning to build ships and to trade, on which the king received heavy duties.

[In the following excerpt, Barbosa describes the customs and social practices of Muslims on the Malabar Coast (the Mappilas) and how they retained aspects of Hindu culture. He also notes the diversity of "Moors" at Indian ports, including Arabs and Persians. As the account below makes clear, the Mappilas did not abandon their previous Hindu customs.]

And in this land of Malabar there are Moors in great numbers who speak the same tongue as the Heathens of the land, and go naked . . . , but as a token of distinction from the Heathen, they wear little round caps on their heads, and long beards. . . . These follow the Heathen custom in many ways; their sons inherit half their property, and their nephews (sister's son) take the other half. They belong to the sect of [Muhammad], their holy day is Friday. Throughout this land they have a great number of mosques. They marry as many wives as they can support and keep as well many heathen concubines of low caste. If they have sons or daughters by these they make them Moors, and often times the mother as well, and thus this evil generation continues to increase in Malabar; the people of the country call them Mapuleres.

[Regarding the diversity of Muslims at Calicut, Barbosa notes the following:]

There are many other foreign Moors as well in the town of Calecut, who are called Paradesis, natives of divers lands, Arabs, Persians, [Gujaratis], and [Deccanis], who are settled here. And the trade of this country is very large, they gathered here in great numbers with their wives and sons, and seem to have increased.

10

ANTOINE GALLAND

The Thousand and One Nights
1717

The Thousand and One Nights, also known as The Arabian Nights, is a popular mix of Persian, Turkish, Egyptian, and Indian folktales, religious legends, and historical anecdotes, which were variously compiled in manuscript form by anonymous editors by the twelfth century. Europeans were largely introduced to the text through the Frenchman Antoine Galland, who in 1704 published the first European translation of The Thousand and One Nights, *based on a Syrian manuscript he found in Constantinople. The story of Sinbad, a sailor from Basra who travels to East Africa and South Asia during the Abbasid caliphate, gives expression to the trials and travails of the quintessential Muslim sailor-adventurer of the Indian Ocean world. How is Islam portrayed as part of this story? What clues might the story offer in terms of understanding the dynamics between Muslims and non-Muslims?*

In the reign of the Caliph Haroun-al-Raschid ... *The Sixth Voyage*
"You long without doubt to know," said [Sinbad], "how, after having been shipwrecked five times, and escaped so many dangers, I could resolve again to tempt fortune, and expose myself to new hardships. I

Muhsin al-Musawi, introduction and notes to *The Arabian Nights*, based on the French translation by Antoine Galland (New York: Barnes & Noble Classics, 2007), 475, 505–11.

am, myself, astonished at my conduct when I reflect upon it, and must certainly have been actuated by my destiny. But be that as it may, after a year's rest I prepared for a sixth voyage, notwithstanding the entreaties of my kindred, who did all in their power to dissuade me.

"Instead of taking my way by the Persian Gulf, I travelled once more through several provinces of Persia and the Indies, and arrived at a seaport, where I embarked in a ship, the captain of which was bound on a long voyage. It was long indeed, for the captain and pilot lost their course. They, however, at last discovered where they were, but we had no reason to rejoice at the circumstance. Suddenly we saw the captain quit his post, uttering loud lamentations. He threw off his turban, pulled his beard, and beat his head like a madman. We asked him the reason, and he answered, that he was in the most dangerous place in all the ocean. 'A rapid current carries the ship along with it,' said he, 'and we shall all perish in less than a quarter of an hour. Pray to Allah to deliver us from this peril; we cannot escape, if He does not take pity on us.' At these words he ordered the sails to be lowered; but all the ropes broke, and the ship was carried by the current to the foot of an inaccessible mountain, where she struck and went to pieces, yet in such a manner that we saved our lives, our provisions, and the best of our goods.

"This being over, the captain said to us: 'Allah has done what pleased Him. Each of us may dig his grave, and bid the world adieu; for we are all in so fatal a place, that none shipwrecked here ever returned to their homes.' His discourse afflicted us sensibly, and we embraced each other, bewailing our deplorable lot.

"The mountain at the foot of which we were wrecked formed part of the coast of a very large island.

"We continued upon the shore in a state of despair, and expected death every day. At first we divided our provisions as equally as we could, and thus every one lived a longer or shorter time, according to his temperance, and the use he made of his provisions. . . .

"I survived all my companions, yet when I buried the last, I had so little provision remaining that I thought I could not long endure and I dug a grave, resolving to lie down in it because there was no one left to inter me.

"But it pleased Allah once more to take compassion on me, and put it in my mind to go to the bank of the river which ran into the great cavern. Considering its probable course with great attention, I said to myself: 'This river, which runs thus underground, must somewhere have an issue. If I make a raft, and leave myself to the current, it will convey me to some inhabited country, or I shall perish. If I drown, I lose nothing, but only change one kind of death for another.'

"I immediately went to work upon large pieces of timber and cables, for I had choice of them, and tied them together so strongly that I soon made a very solid raft. When I had finished, I loaded it with rubies, emeralds, ambergris, rock-crystal, and bales of rich stuffs. Having balanced my cargo exactly, and fastened it well to the raft, I went on board with two oars that I had made, and leaving it to the course of the river, resigned myself to the will of Allah.

"As soon as I entered the cavern I lost all light, and the stream carried me I knew not where. Thus I floated some days in perfect darkness, and once found the arch so low, that it very nearly touched my head, which made me cautious afterward to avoid the like danger. All this while I ate nothing but what was just necessary to support nature; yet, notwithstanding my frugality, all my provisions were spent. Then a pleasing stupor seized upon me. I cannot tell how long it continued; but when I revived, I was surprised to find myself in an extensive plain on the brink of a river, where my raft was tied, amidst a great number of Negroes. I got up as soon as I saw them, and saluted them. They spoke to me, but I did not understand their language. I was so transported with joy, that I knew not whether I was asleep or awake; but being persuaded that I was not asleep, I recited aloud the following words in Arabic: 'Call upon the Almighty, He will help thee; you need not perplex yourself about anything else: shut your eyes, and while you are asleep, Allah will change your bad fortune into good.'

"One of the blacks, who understood Arabic, hearing me speak thus, came toward me and said: 'Brother, be not surprised to see us; we are inhabitants of this country, and came here today to water our fields. We observed something floating upon the water, and, perceiving your raft, one of us swam into the river and brought it here, where we fastened it, as you see, until you should awake. Pray tell us your history, for it must be extraordinary; how did you venture yourself into this river, and whence did you come?' I begged of them first to give me something to eat, and then I would satisfy their curiosity. They gave me several sorts of food, and when I had satisfied my hunger, I related all that had befallen me, which they listened to with attentive surprise. As soon as I had finished, they told me, by the person who spoke Arabic and interpreted to them what I said, that it was one of the most wonderful stories they had ever heard, and that I must go along with them, and tell it to their king myself; it being too extraordinary to be related by any other than the person to whom the events had happened.

"They immediately sent for a horse, which was brought in a little time; and having helped me to mount, some of them walked before to show the way, while the rest took my raft and cargo and followed.

"We marched till we came to the capital of Serendib [Sri Lanka], for it was in that island I had landed. The blacks presented me to their king; I approached his throne, and saluted him as I used to do the Kings of the Indies; that is to say, I prostrated myself at his feet. The prince ordered me to rise, received me with an obliging air, and made me sit down near him. . . .

"The capital of Serendib stands at the end of a fine valley, in the middle of the island, encompassed by mountains the highest in the world. Rubies and several sorts of minerals abound. . . . All kinds of rare plants and trees grow there, especially cedars and cocoa-nut. There is also a pearl-fishing in the mouth of its principal river; and in some of its valleys are found diamonds. I made, by way of devotion, a pilgrimage to the place where Adam was confined after his banishment from Paradise, and had the curiosity to go to the top of the mountain.

"When I returned to the city, I prayed the king to allow me to return to my own country, and he granted me permission in the most honorable manner. He would force a rich present upon me; and when I went to take my leave of him, he gave me one much more considerable, and at the same time charged me with a letter for the Commander of the Faithful, our sovereign, saying to me: 'I pray you give this present from me, and this letter, to the Caliph, and assure him of my friendship.' I took the present and letter and promised his majesty punctually to execute the commission with which he was pleased to honor me.

"The letter from the King of Serendib was written on the skin of a certain animal of great value, because of its being so scarce, and of a yellowish color. The characters of this letter were of azure and the contents as follows:

"'The King of the Indies, before whom march one hundred elephants, who lives in a palace that shines with one hundred thousand rubies, and who has in his treasury twenty thousand crowns enriched with diamonds, *to Caliph Haroun-al-Raschid*:

Though the present we send you be inconsiderable, receive it, however, as a brother, in consideration of the hearty friendship which we bear for you, and of which we are willing to give you proof. We desire the same part in your friendship, considering that we believe it to be our merit, being of the same dignity with yourself. We conjure you this in quality of a brother. Adieu.'

"The present consisted, first, of a single ruby made into a cup, about half a foot high, an inch thick, and filled with round pearls of half a drachma each. Secondly, the skin of a serpent, whose scales were as large as an ordinary piece of gold, and had the virtue to preserve from sickness those who lay upon it. Thirdly, fifty thousand drachmas of the best wood of aloes, with thirty grains of camphire as big as pistachios. And, fourthly, a female slave of ravishing beauty, whose apparel was all covered over with jewels.

"The ship set sail, and after a very successful navigation we landed at Basra, and from there I went to Bagdad, where the first thing I did was to acquit myself of my commission.

"I took the king of Serendib's letter and went to present myself at the gate of the Commander of the Faithful.

"The caliph was much pleased with my account. 'The wisdom of that king,' said he, 'appears in his letter, and after what you tell me, I must confess, that his wisdom is worthy of his people, and his people deserve so wise a prince.' Having spoken thus, he dismissed me, and sent me home with a rich present."

Sinbad left off, and his company retired; and next day they returned to hear the relation of his seventh and last voyage.

11

FRANÇOIS BERNIER

Travels in the Mogul Empire

ca. 1668

Starting in 1656, the French doctor François Bernier spent much of his life traveling across Asia. He journeyed to Egypt, through Persia, and then to India. He chronicled his ten-year stay in Persia and India in a number of books, including The History of the Late Rebellion in the State of the Great Mogol. *His descriptions, like those of Ibn Battuta, Abd-er-Razzak, and other travelers, are remarkable in their detail, especially his observations of everyday life in Mughal (Mogul) India.*

François Bernier, *Travels in the Mogul Empire, A.D. 1656–1668* (London: Oxford University Press, 1916), 241–51.

It is about forty years ago that Chah-Jehnan [Shah Jahan], father of the present Great Mogol, Aureng-Zebe [Aurangzeb], conceived the design of immortalizing his name by the erection of a city near the site of the ancient Delhi. . . . Here he resolved to fix his court, alleging as the reason for its removal from Agra, that the excessive heat to which that city is exposed during the summer rendered it unfit for the residence of a monarch. . . .

Delhi, then, is an entirely new city, situated in a flat country, on the banks of the [Yamuna], a river which may be compared to the Loire, and built on one bank. . . . Excepting the side where it is defended by the river, the city is encompassed by walls of brick. . . .

The walls of the citadel, as to their antique and round towers, resemble those of the city, but being partly of brick, and partly of red stone which resembles marble, they have a better appearance. The walls of the fortress likewise excel those of the town in height, strength and thickness, being capable of admitting small [cannons], which are pointed toward the city. . . .

Next to the garden is the great royal square, faced on one side by the gates of the fortress, and on the opposite side of which terminates the two most considerable streets of the city.

The tents of such [princes] as are in the King's pay, and whose weekly turn it is to mount guard, are pitched in this square; those petty sovereigns having an insuperable objection to be enclosed within walls. . . .

In this place also at break of day they exercise the royal horses, which are kept in a spacious stable not far distant. . . .

Here too is held a bazaar or market for an endless variety of things; which like the Pont-neuf at Paris, is the rendezvous for all sorts of mountebanks [charlatans] and jugglers. Here, likewise, the astrologers resort, both Mahometan [Muslim] and Gentile. These wise doctors remain seated in the sun, on a dusty piece of carpet, handling some old mathematical instruments, and having open before them a large book which represents the signs of the zodiac. In this way they attract the attention of the passengers, and impose upon the people, by whom they are considered as so many infallible oracles. They tell a poor person his fortune for a payssa (which is worth about one sol); and after examining the hand and face of the applicant, turning over the leaves of the large book, and pretending to make certain calculations, these impostors decide upon the Sahet or propitious moment of commencing the business he may have in hand. . . . The ignorant and infatuated people really believe that the stars have an influence which the astrologers can control.

I am speaking only of the poor bazaar-astrologers. Those who frequent the court of the grandees are considered by them eminent doctors, and become wealthy. The whole of Asia is degraded by the same superstition. Kings and nobles grant large salaries to these crafty diviners, and never engage in the most trifling transaction without consulting them. They read whatever is written in heaven; fix up the Sahet, and solve every doubt by opening the Koran.

3

Islamic Law, the Qur'an, and Hadith

Muslims across the Indian Ocean world were variously guided by Shari'a—Islamic codes of conduct, or law, that were principally grounded in the ulema's interpretations of the Qur'an and Hadith (the traditions and sayings of the early Muslim community, also called the Sunna). In a number of ways, however, Muslims' behavior was also shaped by local customs and political conditions. Legal specialists of the Shafi'i school dominated much of Islamic jurisprudence in the region. Hanafi legal scholars from Central Asia were also influential, while Maliki scholars were mostly limited to parts of Arabia (in addition to North Africa, where Ibn Battuta received his basic knowledge). The documents in this chapter include legal treatises that discuss the foundations of Islamic law and different perspectives regarding civil society, gender, and the treatment of slaves. Nevertheless, we begin with the *Azzan*, or call to prayer, heard five times daily according to tradition, which captures the essence of what all Muslims should believe and practice—namely, the *shahada* (profession of faith) and ritual prayer.

12

The Azzan

ca. 622

The Azzan, *or call to prayer, articulates the most basic principle of Islam—that there is only one god, Allah, whose messenger is Muhammad. Prayer is a way of affirming one's submission to Allah. According*

Sahih al-Bukhari, vol. 1, book 11, Hadith, 577–81. www.sunnah.com/bukhari/10.

to both Sunni and Shi'a tradition, the Azzan was first made in the seventh century by Bilal Ibn Rabah, Islam's first mu'azzin (the person who makes the call). It is heard across the ummah five times a day and is rendered, like a song, in various ways (with only slight differences in the wording among Sunni and Shi'a), depending on the sensibilities and training of the person doing it. In carrying out the Azzan, the mu'azzin affirms and reaffirms the unity and continuity of the ever-growing, ever-changing ummah.

The sound of the Azzan is familiar across the Muslim world. The prayer itself (conducted five times daily and called salat in Arabia and namaz in South Asia) is a social act of piety wherein one prostrates oneself facing Mecca. The first line is repeated four times, the next five lines are repeated twice, and the last line is said once. See Document 19 for a discussion of the Azzan from the Hadith, as narrated by Ibn 'Umar.

Allah-u-Akbar
Ash-hadu an-la ilaha illa-Allah
Asha-hadu anna Muhammadan-Rasul Allah
Hayya 'ala s-salah
Hayya 'ala l'-falah
Allah-u-Akbar
La illaha illa-Allah

Allah is great
I bear witness that there is no god but Allah
I bear witness that Muhammad is Allah's Messenger
Come to prayer
Come to success
Allah is great
There is no god but Allah

13

FAKHR UD-DIN AL-RAZI

An Encyclopedia of the Sciences

ca. 1175

Fakhr ud-din al-Razi, a twelfth-century jurist and theologian, offers a clear outline of the bases of Muslim jurisprudence. His work appeared in Jami' ul-'Ulum *(An Encyclopedia of the Sciences). Al-Razi lived for a time in the Punjab region during the conquest of northern India, under the patronage of the Ghurid sultans Ghiyath ud-din and Muhammad Ibn Sam.*

The first basis is the knowledge of the evidences of the mandates of the Holy Law. These are four—Allah's book, the Sunna of the Prophet of Allah, the consensus of the community, and analogy. The explanation of the Qur'an and the Sunna of the Prophet has been adduced. It is evident that when the Prophethood of Muhammad became acknowledged and the truth of what he said established, whatever he indicated by his practice and gave witness as truth is right and true. Further the consensus of the community is established by the fact that Allah Most High said, "He who resists the Prophet after the right way has been made clear to him, we will cause him to suffer the fate he has earned. We shall cause him to burn in Hell. What an evil fate!" Since in the light of this verse it is forbidden and unlawful to follow other than the way of the believers, it follows that it is right and true to follow the way of the believers. Likewise, the Prophet said, "My community will not agree upon an error." [If a mistake had been possible in the consensus of the community, it would have been a deviation from the right path], for then the falseness of this tradition would necessarily follow and this is untrue. But what analogy proves is that the events and vicissitudes of life are infinite and the evidences are finite. To affirm the infinite by means of the finite is absurd; therefore it is evident that there is no avoiding analogy and the employment of one's own opinion [*ijtihad*]. Therefore it is evident that all the four sources are right and true. . . .

Fakhr ud-din al-Rāzī, *Jāmi' ul-'Ulūm* (*An Encyclopedia of the Sciences*), 11th ed. (Bombay: n.p., 1908), 8–9.

There are ten conditions of legal interpretation.

The first is knowledge of Allah's Holy Book because it is a foundation of the knowledge of the mandates of the Shari'a. But it is not a necessary condition that there should be knowledge of the whole Book but only of those verses which are relevant to the mandates of the Holy Law—to wit, to the number of five hundred verses, and no more. It is necessary that these verses should be in the *mujtahid*'s [interpreter of the faith's] memory in such a way that when need of them arises it is possible to attain his object in the knowledge of one of the mandates of the Holy Law.

The second condition is knowledge of the traditions of the Prophet. In the same way as in the knowledge of the word of Allah, where there was no need to know all, but only to remember some points, so it is with the traditions of the Prophet.

Thirdly, it is a condition of legal interpretation that one should know the abrogating and the abrogated portions of the Qur'an and of the Sunna, so that no error should occur in legal interpretation.

Fourth, one should discriminate between the reason why a tradition is valid or invalid and discern the true from the false.

Fifth, the interpreter of the law should be aware of the problems which have been resolved among the *ummah* because if he is not aware of them he may deliver a formal legal opinion which is against the consensus of the community and this is not permissible.

Sixth, knowledge of the manner of arranging Shari'a evidence in a way which will bring forth a conclusion and distinguish truth from error in that conclusion. The interpreter of the law should know what are the occasions of error and how many there are, so that he may avoid them.

The seventh is awareness of the fundamentals of the faith—knowledge of creation, of the unity of Allah, and of His freedom from sin and vice. The interpreter of the law should know that the Creator is eternal, knowing, and powerful.

The eighth and ninth are that he should know lexicography and grammar to such an extent that by their means he can know the intentions of Allah and of the Prophet in the Qur'an and the Traditions.

The tenth condition is knowledge of the sciences of the bases of jurisprudence and comprehension of what is commanded and what is prohibited, the universal and the particular.

14

MAULANA BURHAN UD-DIN MARGHINANI

Guidance

ca. 1195

The Hidaya *(Guidance) was written by the twelfth-century jurist Maulana Burhan ud-din Marghinani, of Transoxania in Central Asia.
According to the predominant school of law in northern India, the
Hanafi, the* Hidaya *is considered the standard exposition of the principles
of jurisprudence. It starts with the compulsory religious duties ('ibadat)
of ritual purification, prayer, alms, fasting, and pilgrimage. It also covers
a number of principles of Islamic law, including those related to marriage, divorce, adultery, manumission of slaves, the treatment of infidels,
loans, gifts, rules of evidence, and wills. The following excerpts refer to the
alms tax (zakat) and its disbursement, polygamy, and the testimony of
dhimmis (zimmis).*

Alms-giving is an ordinance of Allah, incumbent upon every person who
is free, sane, adult, and a Muslim, provided he be possessed, in full property, of such estate or effects as are termed in the language of the law a
minimum, and that he has been in possession of the same for the space
of one complete year. . . . The reason for this obligation is found in the
word of Allah, who has ordained it in the Qur'an, saying, "Bestow alms."
The same injunction occurs in the traditions, and it is moreover univer
sally admitted. The reason for freedom being a requisite condition is
that this is essential to the complete possession of property. The reason
why sanity of intellect and maturity of age are requisite conditions shall
be hereafter demonstrated. The reason why the Muslim faith is made a
condition is that the rendering of alms is an act of piety, and such cannot
proceed from an infidel. . . .

    The objects of the disbursement of alms are of eight different descrip-
tions: first, the needy; secondly, the destitute; thirdly, the collector of

---

Maulana Burhān ud-dīn Marghīnānī, *Hidāya*, trans. C. Hamilton (London: W. H. Allen,
1791), 670–71, 690–91, in *Sources of Indian Tradition*, vol. 1, *From the Beginning to 1800*,
ed. Ainslie T. Embree (New York: Columbia University Press, 1988), 404–6.

alms; . . . fourthly, slaves . . . ; fifthly, debtors not possessed of property amounting to a legal minimum; sixthly, in the service of Allah; seventhly, travelers; and eighthly, the winning over of hearts. And those eight descriptions are the original objects of the expenditure of alms, being particularly specified as such in the Qur'an; and there are, therefore, no other proper or legal objects of its application. With respect to the last, however, the law has ceased to operate, since the time of the Prophet, because he used to bestow alms upon them as a bribe or gratuity to prevent them from molesting the Muslims, and also to secure their occasional assistance; but when Allah gave strength to the faith, and to its followers, and rendered the Muslims independent of such assistance, the occasion of bestowing this gratuity upon them no longer remained; and all the doctors unite in this opinion. . . .

It is lawful for a freeman to marry four wives, whether free or slaves; but it is not lawful for him to marry more than four, because Allah has commanded in the Qur'an, saying: "Ye may marry whatsoever women are agreeable to you, two, three, or four," and the numbers being thus expressly mentioned, and beyond what is there specified would be unlawful. Shafi'i alleges a man cannot lawfully marry more than one woman of the description of slaves, from his tenet as above recited, that "the marriage of freemen with slaves is allowable only from necessity"; the text already quoted is, however, in proof against him, since the term "women" applied equally to free women and to slaves. . . .

In all rights, whether of property or otherwise, the probity of the witness, and the use of the word *shahadat* [evidence] is requisite; even in the case of the evidence of women with respect to birth, and the like; and this is approved; because *shahadat* is testimony, since it possesses the property of being binding; whence it is that it is restricted to the place of jurisdiction; and also, that the witness is required to be free; and a Muslim. If, therefore, a witness should say: "I know," or "I know with certainty," without making use of the word *shahadat*, in that case his evidence cannot be admitted. With respect to the probity of the witness, it is indispensible, because of what is said in the Qur'an: "Take the evidence of two just men." . . .

The testimony of *zimmis* [protected unbelievers] with respect to each other is admissible, notwithstanding they be of different religions. Maliki and Shafi'i have said that their evidence is absolutely inadmissible, because, as infidels are unjust, it is requisite to be slow in believing anything they may advance, Allah having said [in the Qur'an]: "When an unjust person tells you anything, be slow in believing him"; when it is that the evidence of an infidel is not admitted concerning a Muslim; and, consequently, that an infidel stands [in this particular] in the same predicament with an apostate.

15

ABU HAMID MUHAMMAD AL-GHAZALI

Revival of the Religious Sciences

ca. 1100

Abu Hamid Muhammad al-Ghazali was a twelfth-century Persian theologian, philosopher, and jurist from Baghdad. Here he delineates the rights enslaved people should expect under Muslim political authority based on the Qur'an and Hadith. Al-Ghazali was one of the few scholars of his time to comment on the rights of slaves.

One of the last injunctions of the Prophet—may Allah bless him and grant him peace—was his saying: "Fear Allah concerning those whom your right hand possesses. Feed them with what you eat, and clothe them with what you wear, and do not assign them to work that is beyond their capacity. Those whom you like, retain; and those whom you dislike, sell. Do not torment Allah's creatures. Allah made you their owner, and had He wished, He could have made them your owners." ... He also said—peace be upon him: "The following shall not enter Paradise: the imposter, the arrogant, the traitor, and he who treats his slaves he owns badly." Abd Allah son of Umar—may Allah be pleased with both—said: "A man came to the Messenger of Allah—may Allah bless him and grant him peace—and said, 'O Messenger of Allah, how many times should we pardon a slave?' The Messenger of Allah was silent, then he said 'Seventy times every day.'" Umar—may Allah be pleased with him—used to

Abu Hamid Muhammad al-Ghazali, *Ihya 'Ulum al-Din* (*Revival of the Religious Sciences*) (Cairo: n.p., 1967), 2:219–21, 279–91.

visit slave owners on Saturdays, and if he found a slave (*abd*) engaged in work beyond his capacity he would release him from it.

Ibn al-Munkadir said: "One of the Companions of the Prophet—may Allah Most High bless him and grant him peace—was beating a slave of his, and the slave began to say, 'I beseech you by Allah. I beg you for Allah's sake,' but he did not pardon him. The messenger of Allah—may Allah Most High bless him and grant him peace—heard the cry of the slave and went to him. When the Companion saw the Messenger of Allah, he stopped what he was doing. The Messenger of Allah said to him, 'When he begged you for Allah's sake you did not pardon him, but when you saw me, you stopped.' The Companion said, 'He is free for the sake of Allah, O Messenger of Allah.' The Prophet said, 'Had you not freed him, the Fire of Hell would have scorched your face.'" . . .

The Messenger of Allah also said: "He who owns a slave girl and protects her [chastity] and acts kindly towards her, then frees her and marries her, shall have two rewards." He also said: "Each one of you is a shepherd and each is responsible for his flock."

In sum, the right of the slave is that his master should share his food and clothing with him, not give him tasks beyond his strength, not look [at] him with the eye of arrogance and disdain, forgive him for his trespasses, and when he is angry with him for some lapse or offense, think of his own sins and offenses against Almighty Allah and his shortcoming in obedience to Allah, and remember that Allah's power is greater over him than his power over his slave.

[The voices of two young female slaves, one owned by Maymun Ibn Mihran and the other by Abu'l-Darda, are articulated in this part of the Ihya 'Ulum al-Din. Both of these women are able to argue their way to freedom by imploring their masters to do what is just and sanctioned in the Qur'an.]

A slave girl of Abu'l-Darda said to him: "For a year I have been poisoning you, but nothing happens to you." He said: "Why do you do this?" She said: "I want to be rid of you." He said: "Go, you are free for the sake of Allah."

Al-Zuhri said: "If you say to a slave: 'May Allah punish you.' Then he is free." Someone said to al-Ahnaf ibn Qays: "From whom did you learn magnanimity?" He said: "From Qays ibn Asim." It was said: "How far did his magnanimity reach?" He replied: "Once when he was sitting in his house a slavewoman came with a roast on a spit, the spit fell from her hand on his son, who was wounded and died. The slave girl was horrified, and he said: 'Nothing will calm this girl but manumission.' He therefore said to her: 'You are free, don't be afraid.'"

"Awn ibn," Abdallah used to say, when his slave disobeyed him: "You are like your master. Your master disobeys his master, and you disobey your master." One day he made him angry, and he said: "What you want is to make me beat you. Go, you are free."

Maymun ibn Mihran had a guest with him, and he told his slave girl to make haste in bringing dinner. She came hurrying, with a full dish; but she stumbled and emptied in on the head of her master Maymun. He said: "Slave girl! You have scalded me." She said: "You who teach what is good and punish people, return to what Allah said." "And what did Allah say?" he asked. She replied: "He said: 'Those who hold back their anger.'" He said: "I have held back my anger." She said: "And those who forgive others." He said: "I have forgiven you." She said: "And more, for Allah also said: 'Allah loves those who do good.'" He said: "You are free for the sake of Allah."

16

ABU AMR UTHMAN

Letter to the Mamluk Sultan of Egypt

ca. 1392

This letter from Abu Amr Uthman, the king of Bornu, an empire in northeastern Nigeria, to the Mamluk sultan of Egypt, al-Malik al-Zahir Sa'id Baruquq, was copied by the Mamluk scribe Abu 'l-'Abbas Ahmad al-Qalqashandi and appears in his Subh al-a'sha fi sina'at al-insha *(The Dawn of the Night-Blind, on the Art of Letter-Writing), completed in approximately 1412. Although most sub-Saharan African captives who were enslaved in the Indian Ocean world came from East Africa, many arrived from the western part of the continent.*

Abu 'l-'Abbas Ahmad al-Qalqashandi, *Subh al-a'sha fi sina'at al-insha*, ed. Muhammad Abd al-Rasul Ibrahim, 14 vols. (Cairo: Dar al-Kutub al-Khidiwiyyah, 1913–1919), in *Corpus of Early African Sources for West African History*, ed. Nehemiah Levtzion and John F. P. Hopkins (Cambridge: Cambridge University Press, 1981), 347–48.

In the name of Allah, the Merciful, the Compassionate. . . .

To the mighty Sultan of Egypt, Allah's blessed land, Mother of the World:

Upon you be peace more fragrant than pungent musk, sweeter than the water of cloud and ocean. . . .

To proceed: We sent to you our ambassador, my cousin, whose name is Idris b. Muhammad, because of the misfortune which we and our vassal kings have experienced. For the Arabs who are called Judham and others have snatched away some of our free people, women and children, infirm men, relations of ours, and other Muslims. Some of these Arabs are polytheists and deviate from true religion. They have raided the Muslims and done great slaughter among them because of a dispute which has occurred between us and our enemies. As a result of this dispute they have killed our king 'Amr the Martyr b. Idris, the son of our father al-Hajj Idris son of al-Hajj Ibrahim. . . . These Arabs have devastated all our country, the whole of al-Barnu, up to this day. They have seized our free men and our relatives, who are Muslims, and sold them to the slave dealers (*jullab*) of Egypt and Syria and others; some they have kept for their own service.

Now Allah has placed the control of Egypt from the sea to Uswan in your hands. [Our] people have been seized as merchandise, so pray send to all your territory, your emirs, ministers, judges, magistrates, jurists, market overseers, that they may look and search and discover. If they find [our people], let them snatch them from [their captors] and put them to the test. If they say: "We are free, we are Muslims" believe them. Do not take them for liars. When the truth is clear to you release them. Restore them to their freedom and Islam. For certain Arabs cause mischief in our land and do not act righteously. They are those who are ignorant of the [Qur'an] and the Sunna of His Messenger. They embellish that which is worthless. So beware of Allah, fear Him, and do not abandon them to be enslaved and sold.

Allah (who is exalted) said, "And the believers, men and women, are protecting friends of one another; they command the right and forbid the wrong." . . .

And [the Prophet] said: "The believer is the believer's brother; he will not wrong him nor forsake him." . . .

"Peace be upon those who follow the right way."

17

AHMAD AL-WANSHARISI

The Clear Measure

ca. 1485

This selection comes from a fifteenth-century compilation of legal rulings by Ahmad al-Wansharisi, a Maliki jurist from North Africa. By the sixteenth century, his multivolume Kitab al-Miyar al-Mughrib *had become widely known and used in the Muslim world, across the Maghreb, and in the Indian Ocean world, including parts of Arabia, Oman, and the Persian Gulf. His ruling regarding slavery is clear: A Muslim cannot enslave someone who is already a Muslim, but he can keep a Muslim slave in servitude if that person became a Muslim after having been enslaved.*

I have been asked about slaves who come from the land of Abyssinia and who profess monotheism and accept the rules of holy law; is it lawful or not to sell and buy them? If they are converted to Islam while subject to the ownership of their master, have the masters the right to sell them or not? And if the Sunna allows the sale of slaves, how is it that the profession of the monotheistic creed, which saves [an infidel prisoner] from death and from punishment in the other world, does not save [him] from the humiliation and the suffering of slavery? Indeed, ownership is an enslavement and diminution of the individual ennobled by the faith. And what is the meaning of the saying of the doctors of the holy law: "Slavery is unbelief [*kufr*]"? Does this apply after one has become a believer?

I reply: If it is proved that a slave was originally an unbeliever of one kind or another—unless he is of [the] Quraysh[1]—and if on the other hand it is not proved that he adopted Islam when he was in his country and a free agent, then once his captors have laid hands on him after conquest and victory, it is lawful for them to sell or buy him, without hindrance. The profession of the monotheistic creed by these slaves does

---

[1] Quraish; polytheistic tribal rulers.

Ahmad al-Wansharisi, *Kitab al-Mi'yar al-Mughrib* (Fes: n.p., 1313 A.H./1896), 9:171–72, in Bernard Lewis, *Race and Slavery in the Middle East: An Historical Enquiry* (New York: Oxford University Press, 1990), 148.

not prevent the continuance of their status as slaves, since slavery is a humiliation and a servitude caused by previous or current unbelief and having as its purpose to discourage unbelief. That is why the slave is deemed "absent" for himself but "present" for his master. When he is liberated, he acquires legal identity and becomes master of his own person. He is then able to own property, to be a judge or witness, or to hold public office.

As to those who profess monotheism and observe the rules of holy law among the slaves arriving from Abyssinia and from other countries of unbelievers and of the House of War, their profession of monotheism does not hinder their sale or their purchase on the basis of their original unbelief and uncertainty, whether their conversion to Islam is previous or subsequent to the establishment of a right of ownership by their master. The doubt is about the hindrance, and doubt about hindrance is of no effect.

Certainly, if it is known that a whole section or community of the inhabitants of a region have adopted Islam or been conquered by Islam, in such a case the way to avoid error would be to prohibit the possession of these slaves.

But if conversion to Islam is subsequent to the establishment of a right of ownership [over the slaves], then Islam does not require freedom, because slavery has been caused by unbelief. This state of servitude continues after the cessation of the unbelief because of its past existence and in order to discourage unbelief.

18

Selections from the Qur'an

ca. 610–632

The Qur'an builds on the revelations of both Judaism and Christianity and incorporates elements of other religious views and practices in the Arabian Peninsula. These include Zoroastrianism, the dominant religion

Translations based largely on Abdullah Yusuf Ali, *The Holy Qur'ān* (Elmhurst, N.Y.: Tahrike Tarsile Qur'ān, 1987). There are six major translations available online at http://quran.com/1, including those by Sahih International and Mohammed M. Pickthall.

of Persia before the coming of Islam, and Hanifism, the belief in an unadulterated form of Abrahamic monotheism espoused by a small group of people in Arabia. According to tradition, the Qur'an was revealed to Muhammad by Allah through the archangel Gabriel over the course of twenty-two years beginning in 610. Muslim believers consider the book to be the final authority on questions of morality and law. The Qur'an recognizes the prophets of the Old and New Testaments and contains specific proscriptions and expectations of all Muslims. It is divided into 114 sura (chapters) made up of ayat (individual verses) of varying length. The following excerpts regarding belief, religious tolerance, gender, and manumission highlight Islam's monotheism, moral standards, and legalistic injunctions. We begin with the complete Sura al-Fatiha, which, along with the Ayat al-Kursi of the Sura al-Baqarah, is considered essential by many Muslims, as these verses articulate much of the essence of Islam.

Belief

Sura al-Fatiha (The Opener) 1:1–7

In the name of Allah, the Merciful, the Compassionate.
Praise be to Allah, The Lord of the worlds.
Most Gracious, most Merciful.
The Master of the Day of Judgment.
Only You do we worship, and only You do we ask for help.
Guide us in the straight Path.
The Path of those upon whom You have been gracious;
not of those against whom You are angry, or of those who go astray.

[It is customary to say "Amin" (Amen) at the end of this sura.[1]]

---

[1] Transliteration of Sura al-Fatiha (The Opener) 1:1–7:
Bismi Allahi arrahmani arraheem
Alhamdu lillahi rabbi alAAalameen
Arrahmani arraheem
Maliki yawmi addeen
Iyyaka naAAbudu wa-iyyaka nastaAAeen
Ihdina assirata almustaqeem
Sirata allatheena anAAamta AAalayhim ghayri
almaghdoobi AAalayhim wala addalleen [Amin]

Sura al-Baqarah (The Cow), Ayat al-Kursi, 2:255

Allah! There is no god but Him; the Living, the Self-sustaining: neither slumber nor sleep seizes Him; to Him belongs whatsoever is in the heavens, and on earth. Who is he that can intercede with Him, but through His good pleasure? He knows that which is past, and that which is to come unto them, and they shall not comprehend anything of His knowledge, but so far as He pleases. His throne is extended over the heavens and the earth; and their preservation is no burden unto Him. He is the High, the Mighty.

Sura al-Baqarah (The Cow) 2:256

Let there be no compulsion in religion: The right course has become clear from the wrong. Whoever rejects Taghut [false gods, idols] and believes in Allah has grasped the most trustworthy handhold which will never break. And Allah is Hearing and Knowing.

Sura al-Baqarah (The Cow) 2:115

To Allah belongs the East and the West; whichsoever way you turn there is the face of Allah. Indeed, Allah is all-Encompassing and Knowing.

Sura al-An'am (The Cattle) 6:97

It is He who placed for you the stars that you may be guided by them through the darkness and the sea. We have detailed the signs for a people who know.

Tolerance

Sura al-Baqarah (The Cow) 2:62

Those who believe, those who follow Jewish scriptures, the Christians, the Sabians, and any who believe in Allah and the Final Day, and do good, all shall have their reward with their Lord and they will not come to fear or grief.

Sura al-Ma'idah (The Table Spread) 5:49

To each of you Allah has prescribed a Law and a Way. If Allah would have willed, He would have made you a single people. But Allah's purpose is to test you in what he has given each of you, so strive in the pursuit of virtue, and know that you will all return to Allah [in the Hereafter], and He will resolve all the matters in which you disagree.

Sura at-Tawbah (The Repentance) 9:5

And when the sacred months have passed, then kill the polytheists wherever you find them and capture them and besiege them and sit in wait for them at every place of ambush. But if they should repent, establish prayer, and give *zakah*, let them [go] on their way. Indeed, Allah is Forgiving and Merciful.

Sura at-Tawbah (The Repentance) 9:29

Fight those who do not believe in Allah or in the Last Day and who do not consider unlawful what Allah and His Messenger have made unlawful and who do not adopt the religion of truth from those who were given the Scripture — [fight] until they give the *jizyah* willingly while they are humbled.

Gender

Sura al-Ahzab (The Combined Forces) 33:35

For the men who willingly surrender to the will of Allah and the women who willingly surrender to the will of Allah, the men who believe and the women who believe, the men who are devout and the women who are devout, the men who are truthful and the women who are truthful, the men who are constant and the women who are constant, the men who are humble and the women who are humble, the men who give charity and the women who give charity, the men who fast and the women who fast, the men who are chaste and the women who are chaste, and the men and women who remember Allah abundantly, Allah has arranged forgiveness for them, and magnificent reward.

Sura al-Nisa' (Women) 4:11–12

The male shall have the equal of the portion of two females; then if there are more than two females, they shall have two-thirds of what the deceased has left, and if there is one, she shall have the half . . . ; this is an ordinance from Allah.

Manumission

Sura an-Nur (The Light) 24:32–33

And marry the unmarried among you and the righteous among your male slaves and female slaves. If they are poor, Allah will enrich them from His bounty. Allah is all-Encompassing and Knowing.

And let those who cannot find a [means to marry] remain chaste until Allah enriches them by His grace. And whoever among those whom your right hands possess [an expression denoting a servant or slave] desires a document [of manumission], write it for them if you know any good in them, and give them some of the wealth that Allah gave you. And do not compel your slave girls to prostitution so that you may seek worldly benefit, if they wish to remain chaste. And if any of you should compel them [into prostitution], then after such compulsion, Allah will be forgiving and merciful [toward them].

Sura Muhammad (Muhammad) 47:4

So when you meet those who disbelieve [in battle], strike [their] necks until you have inflicted slaughter upon them, then secure their bonds, and either [confer] favor afterwards or ransom [them] until the war lays down its burdens. That [is the command]. And if Allah had willed, He could have taken vengeance upon them [Himself], but [He ordered armed struggle] to test some of you by means of others. And those who are killed in the cause of Allah—never will He waste their deeds.

Sura al-Balad (The City) 90:1–20

I do call to witness this City;
And you are a freeman of this City;
And (the mystic ties of) parent and child;
Verily We have created man into toil and struggle.
Thinketh he, that none hath power over him?
He may say (boastfully): Wealth have I squandered in abundance!
Thinketh he that none beholdeth him?
Have We not made for him a pair of eyes?
And a tongue, and a pair of lips?
And shown him the two highways?
But he hath made no haste on the path that is steep.
And what will explain to thee the path that is steep?
(It is:) freeing the bondman;
Or the giving of food in a day of privation
To the orphan with claims of relationship,
Or to the indigent (down) in the dust.
Then will he be of those who believe, and enjoin patience, and enjoin
      deeds of kindness and compassion.
Such are the Companions of the Right Hand.

But those who reject Our Signs, they are the Companions of the
Left Hand.
On them will be Fire vaulted over.

19

SAHIH AL-BUKHARI

Selections from the Hadith

ca. 846

*The excerpts in this selection come from Sahih al-Bukhari's ninth-century
collection of the traditions of the Prophet and his companions describing Muslim rituals, conduct, and social conventions. These traditions
are also used for legal justification by* muftis, *jurists who are trained
in Shari'a and have the authority to issue* fatwas *(legal rulings). They
are each in the form of a statement or recollection made by Muhammad
or one of those closest to him, such as Ibn 'Umar (who would go on to
become Islam's second caliph) and Aisha (Muhammad's later wife and a
major source of the Hadith). Al-Bukhari, a Persian Sunni scholar born
in Uzbekistan, gathered a total of 7,563 traditions, with repetitions, in
98 books. His is the most widely used compilation among the six canoni-
cal Hadith (Sunna) collections in the Muslim world. A central Hadith
is that of the "five pillars" of Islam: the* Shahada *(profession of faith), the
five daily prayers (*salat*), making a pilgrimage to Mecca (Hajj), charitable giving (*Zakat*), and fasting (*Sawm*). By the twelfth century, these
rituals, among a number of others, were largely known and fixed among
the ulema across the growing* ummah *of the Indian Ocean world.*

Sahih al-Bukhari, *The Translation of the Meanings of* (the Hadith), trans. Muhammad
Muhsin Khan, comp. al-Imam Zain-ud-Din Ahmad bin Abdul-Lateef Az-Zubaidi (Riyadh:
Maktaba Dar-us-Salam, 1994). An online version of al-Bukhari's collection and others
may be accessed online at http://www.sunnah.com.

Belief

Hadith, Book 11, No. 1271

Narrated by Ibn 'Umar: Allah's Messenger said: Islam is based on (the following) five (pillars): To testify that *La ilaha ill-Allah wa anna Muhammad-ar-Rasul Allah* (there is no god except Allah and Muhammad is the Messenger of Allah), establishing *Salat* (prayers), paying *Zakat* (charity), to perform *Hajj* (pilgrimage to Mecca), and to observe *Sawm* (fasting) during the month of Ramadan.

Prayers

Hadith, Book 11, No. 578 (Azzan, or Call to Prayer)

Narrated Ibn 'Umar: When the Muslims arrived at Medina, they used to assemble for the prayer, and used to guess the time for it. During those days, the practice of *Azzan* had not been introduced yet. Once they discussed this problem regarding the call for prayer. Some people suggested the use of a bell like the Christians, others proposed a trumpet like the horn used by the Jews, but 'Umar was the first to suggest that a man should call the people for the prayer; so Allah's Apostle (peace be unto him) asked Bilal [Ibn Rabah] to perform the *Azzan*.

Hadith, Book 11, No. 690

Narrated Anas bin Malik: The Prophet (peace be unto him) said, "Straighten your rows as the straightening of rows is essential for a perfect and correct prayer."

[Additional prayers were offered during the last nights of Ramadan.]

Hadith, Book 32, No. 241

Narrated Aisha: With the start of the last ten days of Ramadan, the Prophet used to tighten his waist belt (i.e., work hard) and used to pray all the night, and used to keep his family awake for the prayers.

Hadith, Book 13, No. 8

Narrated Salman-al-Farsi: The Prophet (peace be unto him) said, "Whoever takes a bath on Friday, purifies himself as much as he can, then uses his (hair) oil or perfumes himself with the scent of his house, then proceeds (for the Jumua prayer) and does not separate two persons sitting together (in the mosque), then prays as much as (Allah has) written for him and then remains silent while the Imam is delivering the Khutba, his sins in-between the present and the last Friday would be forgiven."

Hadith, Book 13, No. 60

Narrated Sahl bin Sad: There was a woman among us who had a farm and she used to sow Silq (a kind of vegetable) on the edges of streams in her farm. On Fridays she used to pull out the Silq from its roots and put the roots in a utensil. Then she would put a handful of powdered barley over it and cook it. The roots of the Silq were a substitute for meat. After finishing the Jumua prayer we used to greet her and she would give us that food which we would eat with our hands, and because of that meal, we used to look forward to Friday.

Gender

Hadith, Book 12, No. 2184

Narrated Aisha, Ummul Mu'minin: The Prophet (peace be upon him) said: The divorce of a slave-woman consists in saying it twice and her waiting period is two menstrual courses (qur'). Abu Asim said: A similar tradition has been narrated to me by Muzahir and al-Qasim on the authority of Aisha from the Prophet (peace be upon him), except that he said: And her waiting period ('iddah) is two courses.

Hadith, Book 12, No. 2218

Narrated Thawban: The Prophet (peace be upon him) said: If any woman asks her husband for divorce without some strong reason, the odour of Paradise will be forbidden to her.

Manumission

Hadith, Book 15, No. 1462

Abu Hurayra said: "The Prophet said 'Any man who frees a Muslim slave, Allah will spare from Hell for every limb of the slave a limb [of the liberator]."

Hadith, Book 62, No. 20

Abu Musa said: "The messenger of Allah—may Allah bless him and grant him peace—said: 'Whoever owns a slave girl and educates her, and

is good to her, and frees her and marries her shall have double reward
[from Allah].'"

Hadith, Book 15, No. 4094

The Prophet—may Allah bless him and grant him peace—said: "Your
brothers are your slaves. Allah placed them under your control. Whoever has his brother under his control should feed them and clothe
them out of what he himself eats and wears, and should not impose
upon them labor that overcomes them. Should he do so, then he should
help them."

4

Muslim Polities and Politics

By the late twelfth century, Muslim polities (imperial powers and smaller monarchies) had taken hold across much of the Indian Ocean world. They often competed against one another, as in the Mughal-Bahmani battles in India's Deccan during the sixteenth century. But Muslims also waged war against non-Muslims, as in the battles noted by Ibn Battuta in regard to Java's Sultan al-Malik al-Zahir against Hindu forces (see Document 1) and those fought against Christians with the coming of the Portuguese in the fifteenth and sixteenth centuries, followed by the Dutch East India Company in the seventeenth. The documents in this chapter highlight various Muslim political entities and non-Muslim forces that attacked such polities. While the Portuguese brought an unprecedented degree of violence into the region, scholars have increasingly pointed out that much of daily life was relatively unaffected by their arrival.

20

CHAUNCY H. STIGAND

The Land of Zinj

1913

Chauncy H. Stigand was a British army officer who translated a history of Pate Island (located off the eastern coast of Africa) that was dictated to him by Bwana Kitini, a member of the island's ruling Nabhan royal family. This account, which describes six centuries of Pate political history

Chauncy H. Stigand, *The Land of Zinj: Being an Account of British East Africa, Its Ancient History and Present Inhabitants* (Abingdon, U.K.: Frank Cass, 1913), 29–31.

and the role of Islam starting in 1204, is from the most detailed collection of Swahili oral histories ever recorded. Swahili civilization was primarily Bantu culture from the African coast and its interior combined with Muslim Arab culture and Persian influence.

The beginning of these coast towns, he who first made them was a ruler called Abdul Malik bin Muriani. The date was the seventy-seventh year of the Hejra. He heard of this country and his soul longed to found a new kingdom. So he brought Syrians, and they built the cities of Fate, Malindi, Zanzibar, Mombasa, Lamu and Kilwa.

After that Abdul Malik died, and his sons who reigned did not care for the work of founding towns, and so they left them. Now Abdul Malik's tribe was the Bani Omaiya, and of these fourteen kings reigned. After this the Bani Omaiya dynasty went out and there ruled the Bani al Abbas. The third of this dynasty was Harun al-Rashid, who reigned the year 170 [the Haroon al Rashid of *The Arabian Nights*, who ruled Baghdad].

This sultan heard what Abdul Malik had built in Africa, and he was pleased to call people and give them much wealth [and] sent them to build houses on the coast. The people he sent were Persians.

In the year 601 came the Nabahan [Nabhan] to the coast coming forth from the Oman (Maskat). Now the origin of the Nabahans leaving the Oman is this. In the beginning at Maskat four tribes ruled. First reigned the tribe called the Kharusi. After that they were robbed of their kingdom by the Nabahans. A Nabahan sultan named Iman Muthafar took the kingdom and ruled over the whole of Oman. ["Iman" is the hereditary title of Maskat rulers.] After him came his son Suleiman bin Muthafar, and then the latter's son Suleiman bin Suleiman.

Then occurred a quarrel between the Arabs and the Nabahans among the two tribes of the Henawi and Ghafir. Then the Yorubi fought the Nabahans and they gained strength and defeated the ruling Nabahan. So he went forth and fled away and came to the Sawaheli [Swahili] coast with some of his tribe. . . . He who went to the Sawaheli coast was he who had been Sultan of Maskat.

He landed at Pate and the inhabitants of Pate were those people who had been sent by Khalif Abdul Malik bin Muriani. So he remained in Pate with his people for he had arrived with many men and ships and much wealth. Presently they sent gifts to the chief of Pate and to every big man in Pate they made a present, and even to the small men of the town they gave goods. Then the people, both great and small, perceived the goodness of the Sultan who had come from Maskat.

After he went to Is-hak, the chief of Pate, and asked for his daughter in marriage, and Is-hak gave him his daughter and he married her, and he rested with her the seven days of the honeymoon [the local tradition].

On the seventh day he came forth and went to see his father-in-law. When he came Is-hak said to him, "Your marriage portion is the kingdom of Pate." So Suleiman ruled, and he had a son by that woman and he called him Muhammad. Till the year 625 when Suleiman died, and his son Muhammad bin Suleiman ruled and took possession of all his people, his wealth and his soldiers. It was he who first took the name of Sultan of Pate and this by right, for his father came forth from their country bearing the title of Sultan.

The people of Pate love him much for his own goodness, and because he was a child of the town, for his mother was of their kin. Now Sultan Muhammad remained with them twenty-five years, and then he died leaving three sons, Ahmad, Suleiman, and Ali.

21

An Arabic Account of Kilwa Kisiwani

ca. 1520

The following detailed account comes from an anonymous author whose work was found among the papers of Muhyi al-Din, a qadi from Zanzibar, dating to about 1520. The document discusses the Muslim rulers of the island city-state along the Swahili coast of East Africa. Included are details about the Persian origins of Kilwa's founder and the reign of two of its Muslim rulers, each of whom enforced Shari'a based on the Maliki school of jurisprudence.

Translation by G. S. P. Freeman-Grenville from British Museum manuscript (Or. 2666, British Museum, dated 1867; original from ca. 1520) in G. S. P. Freeman-Grenville, *The East African Coast: Select Documents from the First to the Earlier Nineteenth Century* (Oxford: Clarendon Press, 1962), 34–37.

In the name of Allah, the Merciful, the Compassionate, we ask his Help. Praise be to Allah, praise as wide as his favors, as full as his excellence. . . . May the blessing of Allah be upon our master Muhammad, master of the apostles, seal of the prophets, and upon all his family and companions.

It was His Highness the Sultan who desired me to write a book to inform him of the history of the kings who ruled Kilwa. . . . I hope in Almighty Allah that He may make it a book which will brighten the eyes to read and enlighten the thought to ponder. . . . I have made it consist of an introduction and ten chapters. . . .

Chapter I. The first man to come to Kilwa and found it, and his descent from the Persian Kings of the Land of Shiraz.

Historians have said, among their assertions, that the first man to come to Kilwa came in the following way. There arrived a ship in which there were people who claimed to have come from Shiraz in the land of the Persians. It is said there were seven ships; the first stopped at Mandakha; the second at Shaugu; the third at a town called Yanbu; the fourth at Mombasa; the fifth at the Green Island [Pemba]; the sixth at the island of Kilwa; and the seventh at Hanzuan. They say that all the masters of these [first] six ships were brothers, and that the one who went to the town of Hanzuan was their father. Allah alone knows all truth!

I understand from a person interested in history, and one whom I trust, that the reason for their leaving Shiraz in Persia was that their sultan one day dreamed a dream. He was called Hasan ibn Ali: he was the father of these six men and the seventh of those who left. In his dream he saw a rat with an iron snout gnawing holes in the town wall. He interpreted the dream as a prophecy of the ruin of their country. When he had made certain that his interpretation of the dream was correct, he told his sons. He convinced them that their land would not escape destruction, and asked their advice. They said they left their decision to Allah and his Prophet (may he be exalted!), and to their father.

Their father said he wanted to leave the land and go to another. His sons reported: How can we go? Will the amirs and wazirs and the council agree to your departure? He answered his sons and said: I have a stratagem by which we can escape. Tomorrow I shall summon all of you and the wazirs and amirs and the council. He said to his eldest son: I shall insult you before them all. When you have heard me and show anger, then strike me as if you were filled with rage. I shall become angry on that account and shall make it an excuse to leave the land. In this way, if Allah wills, we shall be able to depart.

Next day he summoned all his sons, and all the wazirs, amirs and the council, and they consulted about such matters as were before them for discussion. The father spoke abusively of his eldest son, who thereupon struck him before them all. His father was angry and said: I will not remain in a land where I have been insulted like this. And the rest of his sons and all the people said: We will avenge you on your son and kill him. He answered: I am not satisfied. And they said: what will you? He replied: only leaving this land will satisfy me.

And they [the sons] agreed to leave with their sultan. He got ready with his household and some of his amirs, wazirs and subjects. They took the road to one of the ports, and, embarking in seven ships, set sail. So they travelled under Allah's guidance to the lands of the Swahili coast, where the ships dispersed, each going to the place already mentioned. This is based on strong evidence, that they were kings in their own country, and is refutation of those who deny it. Allah alone knows all truth!

When we arrived in the ship we went to Kilwa . . . it was an island surrounded by the sea, but that at low water it was joined to the mainland so that one could cross on foot. They disembarked on the island and met a man who was a Muslim, followed by some of his children. It is said his name was Muriri wa Bari. They found one mosque there, said to be the one he is buried in, which is called Kibala.

They asked the Muslim about the country and he replied: The island is ruled by an infidel from Muli, who is king of it; he has gone to Muli to hunt, but will soon return. After a few days the infidel returned from Muli and crossed to the island at low tide. The newcomer and he met together, and Muriri acted as interpreter. The newcomer to Kilwa said: I should like to settle on the island: pray sell it to me that I may do so. The infidel answered: I will sell it on condition that you encircle the island with colored clothing. The newcomer agreed with the infidel. . . . He encircled the island with clothing, some white, some black and every other color besides. So the infidel agreed and took away all the clothing, handing over the island and departing to Muli. He concealed his real intention of returning with troops to kill the newcomer and his followers and to take their goods by force. The Muslim warned the purchasers and said: He is very fond of this island and will undoubtedly return to despoil you and yours of all your possessions and kill you. You must find some stratagem to be safe from his evil intention.

So they set themselves to work and dug out the creek across which in former times men passed at low tide between the mainland and the island. The tide filled it and did not recede again. Some days later the infidel came from Muli to the point from which he was wont to cross. He saw the tide was up; and waited in the usual way for it to ebb until he could cross; but the water remained up and did not go down at all. Then he despaired of seizing the island and was sorry at what he had done. He went home full of remorse and sorrow.

The first king of the land was Sultan Ali ibn al-Husain ibn Ali surnamed Ngu Nyingi [Many Clothes]. And this was the middle of the third century after the flight of the Prophet—peace be upon him! This king ruled Kilwa and then went to Mafia; he liked the island, and so put his son Muhammad ibn Ali, who was known as Mkoma Watu, in charge of it. Muhammad ibn Ali ruled for two and half years, and [was] the first independent king of Mafia after his father died. He ruled four and a half years and then died.

The first man to come to Kilwa ruled forty years. After his death Ali ibn Bashat ibn Ali ruled for four and a half years. He took precedence over his paternal uncles Suleiman ibn Ali, al-Hasan ibn Ali and Daud ibn Ali. When he died his uncle Daud ibn Ali ruled in his stead for two years. Then he went to Mafia to visit his father's grave. He liked Mafia and settled there, and gave his kingdom to his son, Ali ibn Daud ibn Ali al-Husain. He was the last of the seed of the first man to come to Kilwa. Allah knows best!

22

A Journal of the First Voyage of Vasco da Gama
1497–1499

This selection comes from the anonymously written Journal of the First Voyage of Vasco da Gama, 1497–1499, *penned by someone aboard da Gama's ship. Whereas previously maritime trade had been largely free-flowing, the Portuguese, led by da Gama, tried through violence or the threat of violence to control it in ports across the Indian Ocean. The journal describes the first European circumnavigation of Africa, to the*

A Journal of the First Voyage of Vasco da Gama, 1497–1499, ed. E. G. Ravenstein (London: Hakluyt Society, 1898), 1–46.

Cape of Good Hope, and how the Portuguese learned the sea routes to East Africa and India. The following excerpt recounts the initial contact between East Africans and the Portuguese sailors.

In the Name of God, Amen!

In the year 1497 King Dom Manuel, the first of that name in Portugal, dispatched four vessels to make discoveries and go in search of spices. Vasco da Gama was the captain-major of these vessels. . . .

[In March of 1498, we] had cast anchor in the roadstead of the island [near Mozambique] from which these boats had come, there approached seven or eight of them, including *almadias*, the people in them playing upon *anafils*.[1] They invited us to proceed further into the bay, offering to take us into port if we desired it. Those among them who boarded our ships ate and drank what we did, and went their way when they were satisfied. . . .

[The ruler] sent many things to the captain-major. All this happened at the time when he took us for Turks or for Moors from some foreign land, for in case we came from Turkey he begged to be shown . . . our books of the [Islamic] Law. But when they learnt that we were Christians they arranged to seize and kill us by treachery. . . .

On Sunday [March 11] we celebrated mass beneath a tall tree on the island [of São Jorge]. We returned on board and at once set sail, taking with us many fowls, goats and pigeons, which had been given us in exchange for small glassbeads. . . .

During our stay here the King of Mozambique sent word that he wanted to make peace with us and to be our friend. His ambassador was a white Moor and sharif, that is priest, and at the same time a great drunkard.

Whilst at this place a Moor with his little son came on board one of our ships and asked to be allowed to accompany us, as he was from near Mecca, and had come to Mozambique as pilot of a vessel from that country. . . .

In the evening [March 23] we returned to the mainland, attended by the same pilot. On approaching the watering place we saw about twenty men on the beach. They were armed with assegais [a type of sword], and forbade our approach. The captain-major upon this ordered three

[1]A type of straight trumpet.

bombards to be fired upon them, so that we might land. Having effected our landing, these men fled into the bush. . . .

On Wednesday, the 4th of April, we made sail to the north-west, and before noon we sighted an extensive country, and two islands close to it, surrounded with shoals. And when we were near enough for the pilots to recognize these islands, they told us that we had left three leagues behind us an island inhabited by Christians [Kilwa Kisiwani]. We maneuvered all day in hope of fetching this island, but in vain, for the wind was too strong for us. After this we thought it was best to bear away for a city called Mombasa, reported to be four days ahead of us.

The above island was one of those which we had come to discover, for our pilots said it was inhabited by Christians.

When we bore away for the north it was already late, and the wind was high. At nightfall we perceived a large island, which remained to the north of us [Mafia]. Our pilot told us that there were two towns on this island, one of the Christians and the other of Moors.

That night we stood out to sea, and in the morning we no longer saw the land. We then steered to the north-west, and in the evening we again beheld the land. . . .

On the mainland, facing these shoals, there rises a lofty range of mountains [the Usambara Mountains], beautiful of aspect. These mountains we called Serras de São Raphael, and gave the same name to the shoals.

When the vessel was high and dry, two almadians [a small boat] approached us. One was laden with fine oranges, better than those of Portugal. Two of the Moors remained on board, and accompanied us next day to Mombasa.

On Saturday morning, the 7th of the month, and eve of Palm Sunday, we ran along the coast and saw some of the islands at a distance of fifteen leagues from the mainland, and about six leagues in extent. They supply the vessels of the country with masts. All are inhabited by Moors.

On Saturday we cast anchor off Mombasa, but did not enter the port. No sooner had we been perceived than a zavra [small boat] manned by Moors came out to us: in front of the city there lay numerous vessels all dressed in flags. And we, anxious not to be outdone, also dressed our ships, and we actually surpassed their show, for we wanted in nothing but men, even a few whom we had being very ill. We anchored here with much pleasure for we confidently hoped that on the following day we might go on land and hear mass jointly with the Christians reported to live there under their own *alcaide*[2] in a quarter separate from that of the Moors.

The pilots who had come with us told us there resided both Moors and Christians in this city; that these latter lived apart under their own lords, and that on our arrival they would receive us with much honor and take us to their houses. But they said this is for a purpose of their own, for it was not true. At midnight there approached us a zavra with about 100 men, all armed with cutlasses and bucklers. When they came to the vessel of the captain-major they attempted to board her, armed as they were, but this was not permitted, only four or five of the most distinguished men among them being allowed on board. They remained about a couple of hours, and it seemed to us that they paid us a visit merely to find out whether they might not capture one or the other of our vessels.

On Palm Sunday (8 April) the King of Mombasa sent the captain-major a sheep and large quantities of oranges, lemons and sugar-cane, together with a ring, as a pledge of safety, letting him know that in case of his entering the port he would be supplied with all he stood in need of. This present was conveyed to us by two men, almost white, who said they were Christians, which appeared to be fact. The captain-major sent the king a string of coralbeads as a return present, and let him know that he purposed entering the port on the following day. On the same day the captain-major's vessel was visited by four Moors of distinction.

Two men were sent by the captain-major to the king. . . . When these landed they were followed by a crowd as far as the gates of the palace. Before reaching the king they passed through four doors, each guarded by a doorkeeper with a drawn cutlass. The king received them hospitably, and ordered that they should be shown over the city. They stopped on their way at the house of two Christian merchants, who showed them a paper, an object of their adoration, on which was a sketch of the Holy Ghost. When they had seen all, the king sent them back with samples of cloves, pepper and corn, with which articles he would allow us to load our ships.

[2]Alcalde, or local commander and political ruler.

23

HANS MAYR

On the Sack of Kilwa and Mombasa
1505

Hans Mayr was a German traveler who in 1505 described the ferocity of Portuguese attacks on Muslims along the western shores of the Indian Ocean. His account corroborates Zain al-Din's view of Portuguese efforts to seize control of Muslim trade (see Document 7), which were justified on religious grounds. After hearing of the Portuguese devastation at Kilwa and Mombasa, the people of Malindi accepted Portuguese authority.

In the year 1505 . . . Dom Francisco d'Almeida sailed with a fleet of twenty vessels. There were fourteen large men-of-war and six caravels. . . . At dawn on Thursday, 24 July . . . all went in their boats to the shore. The first to land was the Grand-Captain. . . . They went straight to the royal palace, and on the way only those Moors who did not fight were granted their lives. . . . In Kilwa there are many strong houses several stories high. They are built of stone and mortar and plastered with various designs. . . . The town of Kilwa lies on an island around which ships of 500 tons can sail. The island and town have a population of 4,000 people. . . . There are more black slaves than white Moors here: they are engaged on farms. . . . The fortress of Kilwa was built out of the best house there was there. All the other houses around it were pulled down. It was fortified and guns were set in place. . . . The [Moors, however,] are armed with bows and large arrows, strong shields of palm leaves bound with cotton, and pikes better than those of Guinea. Few swords were seen. They have four catapults for hurling stones but do not yet know the use of gunpowder. . . . When the king fled from Kilwa, the Grand-Captain appointed another, a local Moor beloved by all, whom they took in procession on horseback through the town. . . . There are

G. S. P. Freeman-Grenville, *The East African Coast: Select Documents from the First to the Earlier Nineteenth Century* (Oxford: Clarendon Press, 1962), 105–12.

many vaulted mosques, one of which is like that of Cordoba. All the upper-class Moors carry a rosary. . . . When the Grand-Captain went ashore he seized a Moor . . . a member of the royal household . . . and decided to burn the town that evening and to enter it the following morning. But when they went to burn the town they were received by the Moors with a shower of arrows and stones. The town has more than 600 houses which are thatched with palm leaves. . . . Once the fire was started it raged all night long, and many houses collapsed and a large quantity of goods was destroyed.

24

GULBADAN BEGUM

The History of Humayun

ca. 1600

In the sixteenth century, Gulbadan Begum, the daughter of the Mughal Empire's founder, Babur, wrote the Humayun-Nama, *describing her brother Humayun's reign as the second Mughal emperor. In this selection, she recounts the critical Mughal victory at the Battle of Panipat in 1526 and describes the lives of women in the Mughal court: how they acted as counselors and mediators among family members, how they managed property, and how they organized rituals to create a sense of solidarity among themselves.*

In the Name of Allah, the Merciful, the Compassionate.
    . . . After a time his Majesty set out for . . . Qandahar. He was victorious at once . . . and kept its garrison shut up for a year and a half. Then, by the Divine favour and after great fighting and skirmishing, he captured it. Much gold fell into his hands, and he gave moneys and camels

Gulbadan Begum, *The History of Humayun* (*Humayun-Nama*), trans. Annette S. Beveridge (London: Royal Asiatic Society, 1902), 83, 93–98, 128.

to his soldiers and the people of the army. Qandahar he bestowed on Mirza Kamran, and himself set off for Kabul.

His advance camp having been set up, he crossed the hill of Yak Langa, and gloriously alighted in the valley of Dih-i-ya'qub on Friday, Safar 1st, 932 H. [November 17, 1525], when the sun was in Sagittarius. He spent the following day there, and on the next set forth, march by march, for Hindustan. In the seven or eight years since 925 H. [1519] the royal army had several times renewed the attempt on Hindustan. Each time it used to conquer lands and districts . . . when on Safar 1st, 932 H., his Majesty went, march by march, from his glorious encamping in Dih-i-ya'qub towards Hindustan. He conquered Lahore and Sirhind, and every country that lay on his path.

On Friday, Rajab 8, 932 H. [April 20, 1526], he arrayed battle at Panipat against Sultan Ibrahim, son of Sultan Sikandar, son of Bahlul Lodi. By Allah's grace he was victorious, and Sultan Ibrahim was killed in the fight.

His victory was won purely by the Divine grace, for Sultan Ibrahim had a lak [100,000] and 80,000 horses, and as many as 1,500 head of fierce elephants; while his Majesty's army with the traders and goods and all was 12,000 persons and he had, at the outside, 6,000 or 7,000 serviceable men.

The treasures of five kings fell into his hands. He gave everything away. The amirs of Hind represented that in Hindustan it was thought disgraceful to expend the treasure of bygone kings, and that people rather added and added to it, while his Majesty, on the contrary, had given all away.

Khwaja Kilan Beg asked leave several times to go to Kabul. He said: "My constitution is not fitted for the climate of Hindustan. If leave were given, I should tarry awhile in Kabul." His Majesty was not at all willing for him to go, but at last gave permission because he saw him so very urgent. He said: "When you go, I shall send some of the valuable presents and curiosities of Hind which fell into our hands through the victory over Sultan Ibrahim, to my elder relations and sisters and each person of the *haram* ["harem," female space]. You take them. I shall write a list, and you will distribute them according to it. You will order a tent with a screen to be set up in the Garden of the Audience Hall for each *begam* [aristocratic woman, akin to "lady"], and when a pleasant meeting-place has been arranged, the *begams* are to make the prostration of thanks for the complete victory which has been brought about.

"To each *begam* is to be delivered as follows: one special dancing-girl of the dancing-girls of Sultan Ibrahim, with one gold plate full of jewels—ruby and pearl, cornelian and diamond, emerald and turquoise, topaz and cat's-eye—and two small mother-o'-pearl trays full of *ashrafis* [coins], and on two other trays *shahrukhis* [other types of coins], and all sorts of stuffs by nines—that is, four trays and one plate.

"Take a dancing-girl and another plate of jewels, and one each of *ashrafis* and *shahrukhis*, and present, in accordance with my directions, to my elder relations the very plate of jewels and the self-same dancing-girl which I have given for them. I have made other gifts; convey these afterwards.

"Let them divide and present jewels and *ashrafis* and *shahrukhis* and stuffs to my sisters and children . . . and kinsmen, and to the *begams* and *aghas* and nurses and foster-brethren and ladies, and to all who pray for me." The gifts were made according to the list. Three happy days they remained together in the Audience Hall Garden. They were uplifted by pride, and recited the *fatiha* [first chapter of the Qur'an] for the benediction and prosperity of his Majesty, and joyfully made the prostration of thanks.

After Khwaja Kilan Beg had started for Kabul, the Emperor made gifts in Agra to his Majesty Humayun and to all the mirzas and sultans and amirs. He sent letters in all directions, urgently saying, "We shall take into full favor all who enter our service, and especially such as served our father and grandfather and ancestors. If such will come to us, they will receive fitting benefits. Whoever there may be of the families of Sahib-qiran [the Turkic conqueror Timur] and Chingiz Khan [Genghis Khan], let them turn towards our court. The most High has given us sovereignty in Hindustan; let them come that we may see prosperity together."

Seven daughters of Sultan Abu-sa'id came (to Hindustan): Guharshad Begam, and Fakhr-jahan Begam, and Khadija Sultan Begam, and Badi'u-l-jamal Begam, and Aq Begam, and Sultan Bakht Begam. . . .

In short, all the *begams* and *khanams* went, ninety-six persons in all, and all received houses and lands and gifts to their heart's desire. . . .

To the architect, Khwaja Qasim, his Majesty gave the following order: "We command a piece of good service from you. It is this: whatever work, even if it be on a great scale, our paternal aunts may order done in their palace, give it precedence, and carry it out with might and main."

He commanded buildings to be put up in Agra on the other side of the river, and a stone palace to be built for himself between the *haram* and the garden. He also had one built in the audience court, with a reservoir in the middle and four chambers in the four towers. . . . [In describing the gifts offered as part of a Mughal court marriage, Gulbadan Begum describes the following:] nine *tipuchaq* [prized] horses, with jeweled and gold-embroidered saddles and bridles; and gold and silver vessels and slaves, [including] Turki and Circassian and Arus and Abyssinian, of each [race] a royal gift of nine.

25

PIETER VAN DEN BROECKE

On Malik Ambar

ca. 1610

In this document, the seventeenth-century Dutch traveler Pieter van den Broecke describes Malik Ambar, the most prominent Abyssinian ruler in India. Ambar, who was born in Ethiopia and later enslaved, was educated in Baghdad and then served in the Ahmednagar and Bijapur sultanates before becoming the de facto ruler of the latter. Known as an extraordinary military commander and diplomat, a patron of Muslim and Hindu artisans, an innovative agricultural policymaker, and a pious Muslim who taught the Qur'an to his personal guard, he was able to fend off northern Mughal incursions into the Deccan for more than a quarter of a century. While he was traveling through the Deccan, van den Broecke noted how Ambar maintained law and order within the Nizam Shahi dynasty of the sultanate of Ahmednagar, and he made a number of other observations about the ruler.

In the afternoon I went in person to the Melick Ambahaer [Malik Ambar],[1] bringing as presents a Japanese saber and an expensive Japanese kris [a type of dagger]. He liked the Japanese saber but not the kris, because it was decorated with a demon. He gave it back, gave me also a permit for the rest of our people, was very friendly, and hung two expensive *pomerins* [colored cloths] around my shoulders, one made

---

[1]Van den Broecke uses various spellings for Malik Ambar throughout this selection.

W. Ph. Coolhaas, ed., *Pieter van den Broecke in Azie* (The Hague: Martinus Nijhoff, 1962), 1:146–51. With translation assistance by Daniel Prinz.

of gold, the other one of camel's hair; this is the greatest honor one can give a person. He also offered to give me soldiers as a guard and convoy to Golconda.

He had with him an ambassador ... who requested his horse back and compensations for damages done to his people. I told Melick Ambaer that I was now in his land and under his authority; that I had come to his land trusting his word, since he is considered in the whole world as a man who scrupulously keeps his word. If it was his wish that I return the horse, then I would give it up, but not of my free will, indeed very much against it. But if this was not his wish, then the ... soldiers would try to get it by force of arms. He began to laugh and gave the message to the ambassador, who did not like it a bit.

In our company were also some Portuguese *arnegados* [renegades] who said, in Portuguese, "Look at that proud dog," *Vede iste suberbe can!* They came to the Melick to request command of 3, 4, or 5,000 horses. They said: "This dog only comes to spy; watch out." With a friendly face he gave my leave and I rode back to my tent.

The Melick Ambar is a black kaffir[2] from the land of Habessi [Abyssinia] or Prester John's land. He has a ruthless Roman face, and is tall and strong of stature, with white glassy eyes which do not become him. He is a good administrator and was a slave who was sold for 20 ducats in Mocha [in Yemen]. After the death of his master, who was a rich nobleman from the Deccan, he married the nobleman's widow, who did not have much property since the kings of those lands generally confiscate the property of the great lords. He therefore had to take to stealing and robbing, in which he was very successful, and attracted many followers, in the end even to the number of 5,000 horses. He began to dominate and with his robbers maintained himself against the king in an unassailable place where King Nisium Sia [Nizam Shah] could not harm him at all, because this fox was too smart for him; they were at war for many years. Then, because the king was also at war with the Great Mogul, who was trying to fish in this troubled water and become master of the Deccan, [the king] sent for Melick Ambahar and offered him an attractive income if he would return to his obedience and help him against the Great Mogul. The aforementioned Mellick, a cunning man, having noticed the guile and tricks of the king, refused and persisted in his plans, finally having over 8,000 mounted men. He became stronger and got more followers all the time. The king, seeing this, offered peace again. Mellick answered that he would be willing to serve against the

---

[2]A term used to describe East Africans who were non-Christian and non-Muslim, but which is not accurate in this case.

Great Mogul and become the king's eternal vassal, on the condition that the king forgot about the past and agreed to marry Mellick's daughter as his queen. The king consented with approval of his council, married Mellick's daughter with great triumph and magnificence, and after that Mellick came with 8,000 well-equipped cavalry to court, where he was welcomed very much and given another 4,000 horse [a term used in South Asia to designate the size of a person's army] by the king, who thus placed him in direct command over 12,000 cavalry; he was held in high esteem by the king, who gave him considerable income.

At a certain time it happened that the king's wife, who was a white Persian woman, scolded the daughter of the aforementioned Melick Ambahaer with many bitter words, saying that she was only a kaffir woman and a concubine of the king and that her father had been a rebel against the king. The daughter informed her father of this through someone else, and her father then became so angry that he began to plot the murder of the king. He persuaded Mier Abdel Fatj [Amir Abd al-Fath], the king's secretary, to join him, and the latter poisoned the king a short time later with a potion. The king died immediately, leaving a young son whom Mellick Ambaer captured. He then proceeded to bring the whole country under his command.

The king's son is now already 12 years old; he was only 5 when his father died. The Mellick goes to greet him solemnly twice each week as a token of his obedience. The name of the young king is Nisiam Sia [Nizam Shah]. The queen who was the cause of this evil history was also poisoned, shortly after the king her husband.

The aforementioned Melick Ambahar is now the Governor of the whole country, under the pretext that the king is too young. He carries on a vigorous war against the Great Mogul, and he is supported annually by the kings of Golconda, Visiapour [Bijapur], and Baligatte, to wit, by the king of Golconda, whose name is Cote Basja [Qutb Shah], with 6,000 men, by the king of Visiapour, Ebraham Sia [Ibrahim Shah], with 10,000 men, infantry as well as cavalry, by the king of Baligatte, near Goa, with 12,000 men, infantry and cavalry, plus some more from other little kings; this means that he has every year over 80,000 cavalry in his army, which he must keep continually together because of the Great Mogul, who often launches heavy attacks. If the Gatos [Ghats; a mountain range] were not so dangerous to cross, he would have lost this land long ago, and that is the reason why they [Ambar's forces] must be constantly on their guard around this pass through the Gatos.

The aforementioned Melick keeps good order and laws in his country, punishes criminals and thieves severely, and one can travel with gold through his land without any uneasiness. When somebody gets drunk, he has molten lead poured into his throat; nobody is allowed to sell liquor, or even travel with it through the country. The army is very large. . . . At this time of the year it is very cold. In the army camp, called Kerka [Khirki, "rocky town"; the fortress Ambar built near Daulatabad], one can buy everything one can imagine.

The Mellick wanted very much to keep me in his service. He had an offer made to me of 100 pagodas per month and a nice *aldea* [village] or income from a village. There were many Portuguese in his service who had all converted to Islam; some had command over 1,000 horses, others over 3,000 and 5,000; one [was] called Mansour Gaen [Mansur Khan], a half-caste from India.

26

Imperial Edict from Chittagong, Bengal
1666

This revenue document is a late-seventeenth-century sanad *(order) detailing Mughal imperial expansion into Bengal. It discusses the clearing of land for the specific purpose of building mosques. Under the Mughal emperor Aurangzeb, tax-free status was given to any mosque and its affiliates on the condition that approximately 166 acres of forestland be cleared for cultivation. In this way, imperial agrarian policy and Islamic institution building were combined, leading to enormous tracts of formerly forested areas falling under the supervision of mosques.*

Clerks, assessors past and present, headmen, accounts, and peasants of the revenue circles of Sarkar Islamabad, know that:

Shah Zain al-Abidin has made it known that he has many dependents and has built a mosque, where a great many *faqirs* [religious ascetic] and inhabitants come and go. But, as he has no means of maintaining

Imperial edict from Chittagong: Chittagong District Collectorate Record Room, "Kanun Daimer Nathi," Bundle 50, Case No. 3863, in *Islam in South Asia in Practice*, ed. Barbara D. Metcalf (Princeton, N.J.: Princeton University Press, 2009), 387, 389.

the mosque, he is hopeful that the government will bestow some land on him.

Having investigated the matter, the revenue department has fixed the sum of six *shahi dun* and eight *kani* [approximately 166 acres] of jungle land, lying outside the revenue rolls, and located in villages Nayapara and others of *paragana* Havili Chittagong, as charity for the expenses of the mosque as well as charity for the person mentioned above. Once the land is brought under cultivation, the produce of the land must be used for the expenses of the mosque as well as the needs of himself, his descendants, and his dependents. And he must assiduously pray for the survival of the powerful State.

He and his descendants are not required to pay any land revenue or non-land revenue, highway taxes . . . or any other assessments issuing from either the administrative or the revenue branches of government. Nor is he bound to seek a fresh *sanad* each year. Take great care to execute the order.

Dated 2 Rabi I 1077 [AH; September 2, 1666]

5

Conversion and Religious Practice

Islamic conversion did not mean the elimination of all previous religious practices and beliefs. Often it meant adding to or incorporating existing traditions into what was deemed orthodox Islam. As Islam took hold across much of the Indian Ocean world, the religion was transformed in practice and expressed in many different ways—through the retelling of a ruler's conversion, the recitation of devotional poetry or the singing of devotional songs, the infusion of Arabic into local languages, and, of course, the ritual of prayer.

27

MUHAMMAD IBN JUBAYR

The Travels of Ibn Jubayr
1183

A twelfth-century geographer from al-Andalus (Muslim Iberia) describes how he and his companions "died and lived again" multiple times as they survived storms while attempting to reach Mecca by crossing the Red Sea from Africa (from Aydhab to Jeddah). He also gives details about the techniques and materials used in making ships and notes what he deems to be improper conduct among those professing to be Muslims.

Muhammad Ibn Jubayr, *The Travels of Ibn Jubayr: Being the Chronicle of a Mediaeval Spanish Moor*, trans. R. J. C. Broadhurst (London: Jonathan Cape, 1952; repr. London: Jonathan Cape, 2013), 25, 65–66, 69–70.

111

In the name of Allah, the Merciful, the Compassionate; bless and pre-serve our Lord Muhammad, His Family, and His Companions. . . .

The *jilab* [a type of boat] that ply on this Pharaonic sea [the Red Sea] are sewn together, no nails at all being used on them. They are sewn with cord made from . . . the fibre of the coconut and which the makers thrash until it takes the form of thread, which then they twist into cord with which they sew the ships. These they then caulk with shaving of the wood of palm-trees. When they have finished making the *jilab* in this fashion, they smear it with grease, or castor oil, or the oil of the shark, which is best. This shark is a huge fish which swallows drowning men. Their purpose in greasing the boat is to soften and supple it against the many reefs that are met with in that sea, and because of which nailed ships do not sail through it. The wood for these parts is brought from India and the Yemen, as is the coconut fibre. A singular feature of these *jilab* is that their sails are woven from the leaves of the muql tree [a gum tree], and their parts are conformably weak and unsound in structure. Glory to Allah who contrives them in this fashion and who entrusts men to them. . . .

The people of Aydhab use the pilgrims most wrongfully. They load the *jilab* with them until they sit one on top of the other so that they are like chickens crammed in a coop. To this they are prompted by avarice, wanting the hire. The owner of the craft will exact its full cost from the pilgrims for a single journey, caring not what the sea may do with it after that, saying, "Ours to produce the ships; the pilgrims' to protect their lives." This is a common saying among them.

This is the country of Islam most deserving a *hisbah*, and the whip employed should be the sword.[1] . . .

The people of Aydhab belong to a tribe of Sudanese called al-Bujat. Their Sultan is one of their kind and lives with them in the mountains near the city. He will, on occasion, come to meet with the Wali [gover-nor] . . . in order to display his obedience. He is appointed the Wali's deputy in the country and all the revenues, save for a small part, go to him. This race from the Sudan is more astray from the (right) path. . . .

They have no religion save the formal words professing the unity of Allah, which they utter to display that they are Muslim. But behind that are corrupt beliefs and practices that cannot be condoned and are unlawful. . . .

---

[1] *Hisbah* is a punishment by whipping applied in accordance with the Qur'an by an official called the *muhtasib*.

There had been the sudden cries of the sea, the perversity of the wind, the many reefs encountered, and the emergencies that arose from the imperfections of the sailing gear which time and again became entangled and broke when sails were raised or lowered or an anchor raised. At times the bottom of the *jilabah* would run against a reef when passing through them, and we would listen to a rumbling that called us to abandon hope. Many times we died and lived again—praise be to Allah who, in His power and glory, bestowed on us His care, ensuring our protection and sufficiency; praise fitting His kindness, and in solicitation of His continuing favor.

28

PIR HASSAN SHAH (ATTRIB.)

Nizari Isma'ili Qawali Devotional Songs

A Shi'a minority in South Asia called the Nizari Isma'ilis have a rich tradition of Qawali, or Sufi devotional songs. Composed in Gujarati and Hindi, among other languages, and attributed to a number of different Sufi masters (pirs), such songs reflect a mixture of traditions. The Sufi image of a person searching for the divine is both a cultural and religious device used in Qawali that preceded and is shared with non-Muslim devotional traditions. Such Qawali helped in the dissemination of Islam in South Asia.

From His Light He Created the Earth

ca. 1450

From His Light He created the earth and the heavens, suspended Without any support

He revealed His power, manifest in the imam [leader] of the faith.

Patrick Eisenlohr, *"Na't*: Media Contexts and Transnational Dimensions of a Devotional Practice," in *Islam in South Asia in Practice*, ed. Barbara D. Metcalf (Princeton, N.J.: Princeton University Press, 2009), 53–54, 56–57.

Follow the path of the Five Holy Persons [Muhammad, Ali, Fatima, Hasan, Husayn] and have faith in the True Path [Satpanth].

Believers, abide by the Truth and follow the Truth; keep your attention
Firmly on the True Path [Satpanth].

O careless one! Beware of the material world; you will not be misled if
You follow the straight Path.

Countless foolish and helpless souls have blindly wasted their lives.

Pir Hasan Shah has recited this hymn of wisdom (ginan).
Friends! Whoever seeks the Lord, finds Him.

How Tired Are My Eyes

ca. 1625

How tired are my eyes from waiting expectantly;
When will my Lord come?
So that knowing Him to be present before me, I may touch His feet.
Beloved, bowing humbly, I will greet you.

Sweet Lord, I remember your name,
O Lord, I remember your name,
O Master, I remember your name.

My Master, I have been in love with you since childhood;
I am in love with the Lord of the Light.
How can the ignorant possibly understand this?

Sweet Lord, I remember your name,
O Lord, I remember your name,
O Master, I remember your name.

Pir Fazal Shah humbly pleads:
O Merciful One, have mercy on me!
Only your mercy will redeem my honor!
I, your slave, am sinful; You are the Savior.

Sweet Lord, I remember your name,
O Lord, I remember your name,
O Master, I remember your name.

29

The Chronicles of the Kings of Pasai
ca. 1390

Hikayat Raja-Raja Pasai *(The Chronicles of the Kings of Pasai) is a fourteenth-century Malay document describing the Samudera sultanate. The word* hikayat *is a literary term used in the Middle East and Southeast Asia to describe prose that romanticizes certain heroic figures as part of a kingdom's royal chronicles. Among the earliest recorded chronicles in the region, the* Hikayat Raja-Raja Pasai *recounts how the hero figure Merah Silu, a member of the royal family who immigrated to Samudera from Semerlanga and who ruled Pasai from 1275 to 1297, met the Prophet Muhammad in a dream.*

This is the story that has been handed down to us. Once upon a time, in the days when the Prophet Muhammad the Apostle . . . was still alive, he said to the elect of Mecca, "In time to come, when I have passed away, there will rise on the east a city called Samudera. When you hear tell of this city make ready a ship to take to it all the regalia and panoply [splendid display] of royalty. Guide its people into the religion of Islam. Let them recite the words of the profession of faith. For in that city shall Allah . . . raise up saints in great number.

Some time after the Prophet . . . had passed away from this world the elect of Mecca heard that there was a city in the east called Samudera. So the Caliph made ready a ship to take to Samudera all the regalia and panoply of royalty.

A. H. Hill, "Hikayat Raja-Raja Pasai: A Revised Romanized Version," *Journal of the Malaysian Branch of the Royal Asiatic Society* 33, no. 2 (June 1960): 116–17, in Kenneth R. Hall, *A History of Early Southeast Asia: Maritime Trade and Societal Development, 100–1500* (Lanham, Md.: Rowman & Littlefield, 2011), 204.

30

MUHAMMAD MUJIR WAJIB ADIB

The Key to Paradise

ca. 1350

Written in the mid-fourteenth century, these excerpts from a disciple of the Sufi master Nasir ud-din Chiragh, of Delhi, demonstrate how northern Indian Sunni orthodoxy and Sufism were combined in simple teachings to help spread Islam in South Asia. For instance, The Key to Paradise *discusses the spiritual reward of repeating "There is no god but Allah."*

On Praising Allah

It is related that the Prophet said that whoever says every day at day-break in the name of Allah the Merciful and the Compassionate, "There is no god but Allah and Muhammad is His Prophet," him Allah Most High will honor with seven favors. First, He will open his spirit to Islam; second, He will soften the bitterness of death; third, He will illuminate his grave; fourth, He will show Munkar and Nakir his best aspects;[1] fifth, He will give the list of his deeds with His right hand; sixth, He will tilt the balance of his account in his favor; and seventh, He will pass him over the eternal bridge which spans the fire of hell into Paradise like a flash of lightning.

On Remembering Allah

It is reported that a man came to the Prophet and said, "O Prophet of Allah, the obligations of Islam are many. Advise me a little of what I should do, in the letter and in the spirit." The Prophet said, "Keep your lips moist by repeating Allah's name."

---

[1]The angels Munkar and Nakir examined the dead and, if necessary, punished them in their tombs.

Mohammad Mujir Wajib Adīb, *Miftāh al-Jinān*, fols. 4b, 9b–10, 14b, in *Sources of Indian Tradition*, vol. 1, *From the Beginning to 1800*, ed. Ainslie T. Embree (New York: Columbia University Press, 1988), 392–93.

On Saying "In the Name of Allah . . ."

It is reported in the Salat-i-Mas'udi that Khwaja Imam Muhammad Taiyyar reported that on the morning of the Day of Resurrection, the people awaiting judgment will be deserving punishment. The angels will be hauling them up for punishment. They will say to young and old: "Come forth, you who were our followers in the world." Again they will say to the old weak ones: "You are the weak. It may be that Allah will have mercy on your weakness." Then they will go to the very edge of hell. When they say: "In the name of the merciful and compassionate Allah," the five-hundred-year-long fire of hell will avoid them. The Lord of Hell will address the fire: "Why do you not take them?" The fire will reply: "How can I take those who repeat the name of the Creator and remember Him as the Merciful and Compassionate?" Allah's voice will reach them, saying: "They are My servants and the fire is also My servant. He who honors My name, his name too I have held in higher esteem." On the blessings of saying: "In the name of the merciful and compassionate Allah," Allah said: "I have freed everyone in the name of Allah, the Merciful and the Compassionate." Therein are nineteen letters and the flames of hell are nineteen also. Every believer who repeats that rubric, to him Allah will give refuge from the nineteen flames of hell.

31

SHAYKH GISU DARAZ

Women's Devotional Songs

The devotional songs represented in this and the next excerpt reveal Muslim women's daily activities and the ways in which Sufis helped popularize Islam in South Asia. The songs are in Dakhini Urdu, a lyrical, poetic language developed in the Deccan during the sixteenth and

---

Richard Eaton, "Women's Grinding and Spinning Songs of Devotion in the Late Medieval Deccan," in *Islam in South Asia in Practice*, ed. Barbara D. Metcalf (Princeton, N.J.: Princeton University Press, 2009), 90–91.

seventeenth centuries. The chakki *is a grindstone that women used to grind meal; they would sing while they ground the grain.*

Grindstone Song

ca. 1450

The words of this song relate basic Islamic precepts to the different parts of the grindstone and the act of placing the grain on the stone, then grinding and sifting it.

See that our body is also a *chakki*,
And be careful in grinding,
The devil is my *saukan* [co-wife and contender]
Which prevents me from working and tires me.
Ya bism Allah, hu hu *Allah*.

The chakki's handle resembles *alif*, which means Allah;
And the axle is Muhammad, and is fixed there.
In this way the truth-seeker sees the relationship.
Ya bism Allah, hu hu *Allah*.

We put the grains in the chakki,
to which our hands are witnesses.
The chakki of the body is in order
When you follow the *shari'a*.
Ya bism Allah, hu hu *Allah*.

The name of Allah comes from *alif*.
Know that *pirs* and *murshids* [teachers] can direct our lives.
Grind the flour and sift it.
Ya bism Allah, hu hu *Allah*.

Grind the flour and make stuffed *puri* [a type of bread with filling];
Put in it heavenly fruits and sugar,
The seven qualities of Allah must be taken in the body
As the seven ingredients fill the *puri*, oh Sister.
Ya bism Allah, hu hu *Allah*.

Spinning Wheel Song

ca. 1500

In this song, the parts of a spinning wheel are related to Sufi concepts of religious devotion. As in the previous song, this one helped to both disseminate and reinforce basic Islamic principles.

Imagine that your body is a spinning wheel, Oh Sister.
We should get rid of our negligence
And give up worldly differences, Oh Sister.

The tongue is the unspun thread for the message of Allah;
The tongue is the rim of the spinning wheel.
Bring out the thread of breath and show it, Oh Sister.

Both of these memories should be in our throat:
Allah has given us the ability to turn our hand,
And it is that which moves the wheel, Oh Sister.

Faith must be for you what the drive-rope is for the wheel.
Perhaps you know of the two wheels connected by the rope;
Then you will know how the wheel turns, Oh Sister.

As you take the cotton, you should do *zikr-i jail*.[1]
As you separate the cotton, you should do *zikr-i qalbi*,
As you spool the thread, you should do *zikr-i 'ani*.

Zikr should be uttered from the stomach through the chest,
And threaded through the throat.

The threads of breath should be counted one by one, Oh Sister.
Up to twenty-four thousand.
Do this day and night,
And offer it to your pir as a gift.

---

[1] Zikr is a form of devotion based on rhythmic repetition.

Richard Eaton, "Women's Grinding and Spinning Songs of Devotion in the Late Medieval Deccan," in *Islam in South Asia in Practice*, ed. Barbara D. Metcalf (Princeton, N.J.: Princeton University Press, 2009), 91.

32

MUKUNDARAM

Kavikankana Candi

ca. 1590

Kavikankana Candi *is a long poem that was composed in approximately 1590 by the Bengali poet Mukundaram. It suggests larger processes under way in terms of forest clearing and the settling of new lands by Muslims—that is, those who "chant" the Prophet's name. In this selection, the Hindu forest goddess Chandi offers the mighty hunter Kalaketu a kingdom if he will stop hunting and promote her worship. He agrees and, aided by Muslim pioneers, undertakes clearing a large tract of dense forest.*

The Great Hero [Kalaketu] is clearing the forest,
Hearing the news, outsiders came from various lands.

The Hero then bought and distributed among them
Heavy knives, axes, battle-axes, and pikes.
From the north came the Das [people],
One hundred of them advanced.

They were struck with wonder on seeing the Hero,
Who distributed betel nut to each of them.
From the south came the harvesters,
Five hundred of them under one organizer.

From the west came Zafar Mian,
Together with twenty-two thousand men.
Sulaimani beads in their hands,
They chanted the names of their pir [spiritual guide] and the
    Prophet.

Mukundaram, *Kavikankana Candi*, ed. Srikumar Bandyopadhyay and Visvapati Chaudhuri (Calcutta: University of Calcutta, 1974), 299–300, in *Islam in South Asia in Practice*, ed. Barbara D. Metcalf (Princeton, N.J.: Princeton University Press, 2009), 382–83.

Having cleared the forest,
They established markets.

Hundreds and hundreds of foreigners
Ate and entered the forest.

Hearing the sound of the ax,
Tigers became apprehensive and ran away, roaring.

33

Malay Annals

ca. 1550

The story of Muslim conversion by Raja Tengah, an early-fifteenth-century ruler of Malacca, signaled a turning point in the region. Located on the Malay Peninsula, Malacca had become a prominent commercial center for all of Southeast Asia. The ruler's conversion in about 1436 became legendary. The following excerpt is from the sixteenth-century Malay text known as the Sejarah Melayu *(Malay Annals).*

One night the king, Raja Tengah, had a dream. He dreamt that he saw clearly our Prophet Muhammad (Allah's Chosen, may Allah bless him and give him peace): and the Apostle of Allah said to Raja Tengah, "Say 'I testify that there is no god but Allah and that Muhammad is the Apostle of Allah.'" And Raja Tengah repeated word for word what the Apostle of Allah had told him: whereupon the Apostle of Allah said to him, "Your name is Muhammad. Tomorrow, when it is the time for the afternoon prayer, there will come a ship from Jeddah; and from that ship a man will land on this shore of Melaka [Malacca]. See to it that you do whatsoever he tells you." And Raja Tengah answered, "Very well," whereupon the Prophet of Allah disappeared from his sight.

Russell Jones, "Ten Conversion Myths from Indonesia," in *Conversion to Islam*, ed. Nehemia Levtzion (New York: Holmes and Meier, 1979), 136–37.

Then day broke and Raja Tengah awoke from sleep; and he saw that he had been circumcised. And he kept continually repeating, "I testify that there is no god but Allah and that Muhammad is the Apostle of Allah," to the astonishment of all the women-attendants of the palace. And the king's ministers said, "Is this Raja of ours possessed by the devil or is he mad? We had better inform the Bendahara [prime minister] straightaway." So the women-attendants went and informed the Bendahara, and the Bendahara came; and he went into the royal apartments where he found the Raja still repeating continually, "I testify that there is no god but Allah and that Muhammad is the Apostle of Allah." And the Bendahara said, "What language is this that you are talking, Sire?" And the Raja answered, "Last night I had a dream and in that dream I clearly saw the Lord Prophet"; and he told the Bendahara all that he had dreamt. And the Bendahara said, "If your dream was true, Sire, what is there to prove it?" And the Raja answered, "The fact that I am circumcised. That proves the truth of my dream about the Apostle of Allah. And the Apostle of Allah said to me, 'This afternoon, at the time of the 'asar prayers [afternoon], a ship will arrive from Jeddah and from that ship a man will land and say prayers on this Melaka shore. Do as he bids you!'" Then said the Bendahara, "If a ship does arrive at the time of the 'asar prayers, then your dream will be true, Sire. If no ship comes, then of a surety it is the devil plaguing you!" And the Raja said, "I agree." The Bendahara then returned to his house.

And when it was the hour of 'asar, a ship arrived from Jeddah and proceeded to anchor. And from this ship a makhdum [Islamic teacher] disembarked, Sayid Abdul Aziz by name, and then prayed on the shore. And all who saw him were astonished at his behavior and said, "What means this bobbing up and down?" And there was a general scramble to see him, the people crowding together so thickly that there was not a space between one man and another and there was such a disturbance that the noise of it came to the ears of Raja Tengah inside the royal apartments of the palace. And straightaway the Raja set forth on his elephant escorted by his chiefs and he perceived that the makhdum's behavior in saying his prayers was exactly as in his dream. And he said to the Bendahara and the chiefs, "That is exactly how it happened in my dream!"

And when makhdum Sayid Abdul Aziz had finished his prayers, the Raja made his elephant kneel and he mounted the makhdum on the elephant and took him to the palace. And the Bendahara and the chiefs embraced Islam; and every citizen of Melaka, whether of high or low degree, was commanded by the Raja to do likewise. As for the Raja himself, he received instruction in the Faith from makhdum Sayid Abdul Aziz, and he took the title of Sultan Muhammad Shah.

34

ABD AL-RA'UF

Essential Exposition and Clarification on the Visionary Experience of the Dying and What Gladdens Him

ca. 1650

The Sumatran-born scholar Abd al-Ra'uf, one of the most prominent scholars who connected Islam in the Malay-Indonesian world with that in the Arabian Peninsula, describes the experience of dying in this book and also challenges Christians and Jews to avoid straying from the true path.

Let it be known, my disciples, that after I wrote this treatise, I sent a letter to the city of the Prophet, to our enlightened Shaykh in the science of Realities (*'ilm al-haqaa iq*) and in the science of secret details (*'ilm al-daqaa 'iq*), i.e. Shaykh Mawla Ibrahim (al-Kurani), asking (his opinion) about all matters described in the beginning of the treatise . . . ; whether it is correct in the opinion of the (leading) sufis, and whether this matter on the best *dikhr* is discussed in *hadith* books or in any (other) books. . . . After a while, his treatise entitled *Kashf al-Muntazar* was sent by our Shaykh, in which he answered all questions.

Lubb al-Kashf wa al-Bayan lima Yarahu al-Muhtadar bi-al Iyan (Essential Exposition and Clarification on the Visionary Experience of the Dying and What Gladdens Him), MS Leiden University, Cod. Or. 2467, 261–62, quoted in Azyumardi Azra, *Islam in the Indonesian World: An Account of Institutional Formation* (Bandung: Mizan Pustaka, 2006), 138.

6

Pluralism, Syncretism, and Reaction

Muslims expressed Islam in varying ways across the Indian Ocean world, often assuming the characteristics and traditions of the societies into which the religion was introduced. They practiced their faith alongside existing religions, including Hinduism, Buddhism, Christianity, Judaism, Zoroastrianism, and various spiritual practices including polytheism and ancestral veneration. Combining existing religious traditions with Islam produced different kinds of syncretism, which in turn led to religious reactions by Muslims who considered themselves practitioners of a pure, undiluted, orthodox form of Islam. This chapter includes a range of documents that express religious pluralism, syncretism, and reactions to Islam as practiced by Muslims in this vast region.

35

AMIR KHUSRAW

Lovers of God

ca. 1300

Ghazals are a form of South Asian poetry consisting of couplets and a refrain. The one included here was written by the fourteenth-century Indian Sufi poet, historian, and musician Amir Khusraw, who was a spiritual disciple of Nizam ud-din Auliya. Khusraw is known as the originator of Qawali—Sufi devotional songs. Sufis such as Khusraw were often opposed by ulema, who saw their views and practices as a

Kulliyāt-i ghazalīyāt-i Khusraw (The Complete Ghazals of Khusraw), ed. Iqbāl Salāh al-Dīn and Sayyid Vazīr al-Hasan ʿĀbidī, 4 vols. (Lahore: n.p., 1972–1974), 1:362–63, ghazal 190. Translated by Alyssa Gabbay.

corruption of the "true" religion. Khusraw and others, however, believed that spiritual unity underlay religious diversity, as is evident in his ghazals, written in Persian. (Note: The ghazal was not given a title by Khusraw but is taken here from the second line of the poem.)

For me, it matters not whether the love of God is found in the *qiblah*
    or the idol-temple
For the lovers of God, there is no difference between "faith" and
    "unbelief."
Take one step upon your own soul, and the other upon the two worlds
For those who tread the paths of love, there is no lovelier way of going.
Upon the delicate body of Shirin, even a glance weighs heavily
Upon the stout heart of Farhad, even a mountain is light.
See the lover as a holy warrior who's at war with his carnal soul
When he gives up his life in battle, he is no less than a knight.
O Brahmin, give refuge to this rejected one of Islam
Or is there no refuge even before idols for an errant one like me?
How often they say to me: "Go, tie on a sacred thread, O idol
    worshipper."
[But] in the body of Khusraw, which vein is not [already] a sacred
    thread?

36

ABD AL-QADIR BADA'UNI

On Akbar's Tolerance

1595

The Mughal emperor Akbar held power over most of northern India throughout the second half of the sixteenth century. He created a long-lasting administrative bureaucracy by reaching out to his majority Hindu subjects and making them part of his administration. Additionally, he

Badā'ūnī, *Muntakhab ut-Tawārīkh*, 2, 200–201, 255–61, 322, 324, in *Sources of Indian Tradition*, vol. 1, *From the Beginning to 1800*, ed. Ainslie T. Embree (New York: Columbia University Press, 1988), 471–72.

*permitted Hindu-governed territories to retain their own courts and
legal system and repealed several taxes that non-Muslims had previously
paid. His reaching out to Hindus (as well as Buddhists) upset a number
of his Muslim advisers, including Bada'uni, who wrote a detailed
memoir.*

His Majesty . . . passed much of his time in discussing the word of Allah
and the word of the Prophet. Questions of Sufism, scientific discussions,
inquiries into philosophy and law, were the order of the day.

[The] emperor came to Fatehpur. There he used to spend much time
in the Hall of Worship in the company of learned men and shaikhs and
especially on Friday nights, when he would sit up there the whole night
continually occupied in discussing questions of religion, whether fundamental or collateral. The learned men used to draw the sword of the
tongue on the battlefield of mutual contradiction and opposition, and the
antagonism of the sects reached such a pitch that they would call one
another fools and heretics. The controversies used to pass beyond the
difference of Sunni, and Shi'a, of Hanafi and Shafi'i, of lawyer and divine
and they would attack the very bases of belief. . . . [The] *mullas* [Mus-
lim theologians] became divided into two parties, and one party took
one side and one the other, and became very Jews and Egyptians for
hatred of each other [*sic*]. And persons of novel and whimsical opinions,
in accordance with their pernicious ideas and vain doubts, coming out
of ambush, decked the false in the garb of the true, and wrong in [the]
dress of right, and cast the emperor, who was possessed of an excellent
disposition, and was an earnest searcher after truth, but very ignorant
and mere novice, and used to the company of infidels, and base persons,
into perplexity, till doubt was heaped upon doubt, and he lost all defi-
nite aim, and the straight wall of clear law and firm religion was broken
down, so that after five or six years not a trace of Islam was left in him:
and everything was turned topsy-turvy. . . .

And *samanas* [Hindu or Buddhist ascetics] and *brahmins* [upper-caste
Hindus] who as far as the matter of private interviews is concerned gained
the advantage over everyone in attaining the honor of interviews with His
Majesty, and in associating with him, and were in every way superior in
reputation to all learned and trained men for their treatises on morals,
and on physical and religious sciences, and in ecstasies, and stages of
spiritual progress and human perfections brought forward proofs, based
on reason and traditional testimony, for the truth of their own, and the

fallacy of our religion, and inculcated their doctrine with such firmness and assurance, that they affirmed mere imaginations as though they were self evident facts. . . . And the Resurrection, and Judgment, and other details and traditions, of which the Prophet was the repository, he laid all aside. And he made his courtiers continually listen to those revilings and attacks against our pure and easy, bright and holy faith. . . .

[At] one time a Brahmin, named Debi, who was one of the interpreters of the Mahabharata . . . instructed His Majesty in the secrets and legends of Hinduism, in the manner of worshipping idols, the fire, the sun and stars, and of revering the chief gods of these unbelievers, such as Brahma, Mahadev [Shiva], Bishn [Vishnu], Kishn [Krishna], Ram, and Mahama (whose existence as sons of the human race is a supposition, but whose nonexistence is a certainty, though in their idle belief they look on some of them as gods, and some as angels). His Majesty, on hearing further how much people of the country prized their institutions, began to look upon them with affection. . . .

Sometimes again it was Shaikh Taj ud-din whom he sent for . . . and His Majesty listened the whole night to his Sufic obscenities and follies. The shaikh, since he did not in any great degree feel himself bound by the injunctions of the law, introduced arguments concerning the unity of existence, such as idle Sufis discuss, and which eventually lead to license and open heresy. . . .

Learned monks also from Europe, who are called Padre [Father], and have an infallible head, called Papa [Pope], who is able to change religious ordinances as he may deem advisable for the moment, and to whose authority kings must submit, brought the Gospel, and advanced proofs for the Trinity. His Majesty firmly believed in the truth of the Christian religion, and wishing to spread the doctrines of Jesus, ordered Prince Murad to take a few lessons in Christianity under good auspices, and charged Abu'l Fazl to translate the Gospel. . . .

Fire worshippers also came from [Novsari] in Gujarat, proclaimed the religion of Zardusht [Zarathustra] as the true one, and declared reverence to fire to be superior to every other kind of worship. They also attracted the emperor's regard, and taught him the peculiar terms, the ordinances, the rites and ceremonies of the Kaianians [a pre-Muslim Persian dynasty]. [He] ordered that the sacred fire should be made over to the charge of Abu'l Fazl, and that after the manner of the kings of Persia, in whose temples blazed perpetual fires, he should take care it was never extinguished night or day, for that it is one of the signs of Allah. . . .

His Majesty also called some of the yogis, and gave them at night private interviews, inquiring into abstract truths; their articles of faith;

their occupation; the influence of pensiveness; their several practices
and usages; the power of being absent from the body; or into alchemy,
physiognomy, and the power of omnipresence of the soul.

*[Bada'uni notes the influence of Zoroastrian religious practices on
Akbar's variant of Islam, Din-i-ilhai (Divine Faith). Short-lived in practice, Akbar's ideas are contained in scattered writings by various court
chroniclers. Din-i-ilhai was monotheistic and Hindu in sensibility, but it
also incorporated Shi'a ideas in terms of the* mujtahid *(interpreter of the
faith) and borrowed certain Zoroastrian rituals.]*

A second order was given that the sun should be worshiped four times a
day, in the morning and evening, and at noon and midnight. His Majesty
had also one thousand and one Sanskrit names for the sun collected,
and read them daily at noon, devoutly turning toward the sun; he then
used to get hold of both ears, and turning himself quickly round about,
used to strike the lower ends of his ears with his fists. He also adopted
several other practices connected with sun-worship.

37

SHAIKH AHMAD SIRHINDI

Collected Letters

ca. 1600

*The Letters (*Maktubat*) of Shaikh Ahmad Sirhindi to his disciples during the early seventeenth century is one of the classics of Indo-Muslim
religious literature. Sirhindi was the leader of the opposition to Akbar's
lack of enforcement of Shari'a in India. He was against not only Shi'a
Muslims and Sufis, who he believed had gone astray, but also "wicked
ulema."*

Shaikh Ahmad Sirhindi, *Maktubat*, fols. 52–53b, in *Sources of Indian Tradition*, vol. 1,
From the Beginning to 1800, ed. Ainslie T. Embree (New York: Columbia University
Press, 1988), 429–30.

Against Rulers Misled by Wicked Ulema

The sultan in relation to the world is like the soul in relation to the body. If the soul is healthy, the body is healthy, and if the soul is sick, the body is sick. The integrity of the ruler means the integrity of the world; his corruption, the corruption of the world. It is known what has befallen the people of Islam. Notwithstanding the presence of Islam in a foreign land, the infirmity of the Muslim community in previous generations did not go beyond the point where the Muslims followed their religion and the unbelievers followed theirs. As the Qur'an says, "For you, your way, for me, my way" [Sura al-Kafirun 109:6]. . . .

In the previous generation, in the very sight of men, unbelievers turned to the way of domination, the rites of unbelief prevailed in the abode of Islam, and Muslims were too weak to show forth the mandates of the faith. If they did, they were killed. Crying aloud their troubles to Muhammad, the beloved of Allah, those who believed in him lived in ignominy and disgrace; those who denied him enjoyed the prestige and respect due to Muslims, and with their feather brained condoled [grieved] with Islam. The disobedient and those who denied Muhammad used to rub the salt of derision and scorn into the wounds of the faithful. The sun of guidance was hidden behind the veil of error and the light of truth was shut out and obscured behind the curtain of absurdity.

Today, when the good tiding of the downfall of what was prohibiting Islam [i.e., the death of Akbar] and the accession of the king of Islam [i.e., Jahangir] is reaching every corner, the community of the faithful have made it their duty to be the helpers and assistants of the ruler and to take as their guide the spreading of the Shari'a and the strengthening of the community. This assistance and support is becoming effective both by word and deed. In the very early days of Islam the most successful pens were those that clarified problems of the Shari'a and that propagated theological opinions in accordance with the Qur'an, the Sunna, and the consensus of the community, so that such errors and innovations as did appear did not lead people astray and end in their corruption. This role is peculiar to the orthodox ulema who should always look to the invisible world.

Worldly ulema whose worldly aspirations are their religion—indeed their conversation is a fatal poison and their corruption is contagious. . . . In the generation before this, every calamity that appeared arose from the evil desires of these people. They misled rulers. The seventy-two sects who went on the road of error were lost because the ruler enforced his errors on others and the majority of the so-called ignorant Sufis of this time upheld the decisions of the wicked ulema—their corruption was also contagious. Obviously, if some, notwithstanding assistance of every kind, commit an error, and a schism occurs in Islam, that error should be reprehended. But these hateful people of little capital always wish to enroll themselves among the helpers of Islam and to beg importunately. . . . These disobedient people worm their way into the confidence of the generous and consider themselves to be like heroes. . . . It is hoped that in these times, if Allah wills, the worthy will be honored with royal company.

38

DARA SHIKOH

Dara Shikoh, on His Pantheism

The spirit of Akbar's openness with regard to Islam and other religions was carried on by his great-grandson Dara Shikoh. He studied Hindu philosophy and was a follower of the Qadiriyyah Sufi order. His pantheism (the view that Allah and the universe are one and the same) interwove Muslim mysticism with aspects of Hinduism, provoking a strong reaction among adherents of Muslim orthodoxy in South Asia. Shikoh's own brother Aurangzeb condemned him as a heretic and had him executed. The excerpts in this document illustrate Shikoh's spiritual view, his efforts to find common ground between Islam and Hinduism, and his forthright stance against religious orthodoxy and dogmatism.

Dārā Shikōh, *Risāla-i-Haqq-Numā*, 24, 26, and *Journal of Royal Asiatic Society of Bengal* 5, no. 1 (n.d.): 168, in *Sources of Indian Tradition*, vol. 1, *From the Beginning to 1800*, ed. Ainslie T. Embree (New York: Columbia University Press, 1988), 472–73.

The Secret of Unity
ca. 1650

Here is the secret of unity (*tawhid*), O friend, understand it;
Nowhere exists anything but Allah.
All that you see or know other than Him,
Certainly is separate in name, but in essence one with Allah.

Like an ocean is the essence of the Supreme Self,
Like forms in water are all souls and objects;
The ocean heaving and stirring within,
Transforms itself into drops, waves and bubbles.

So long as it does not realize its separation from the ocean,
The drop remains a drop:
So long he does not know himself to be the Creator,
The created remains a created.

O you, in quest of Allah, you seek Him everywhere,
But you are indeed Allah, not apart from Him!
Already in the midst of the boundless ocean,
Your quest resembles the search of a drop for the ocean!

Paradise
ca. 1650

Paradise is there where no *mulla* exists—
Where the noise of his discussions and debate is not heard.
May the world become free from the noise of *mulla*,
And none should pay any heed to his decrees!
In the city where a *mulla* resides,
No wise man ever stays.

Dārā Shikōh, *Risāla-i-Haqq-Numā*, 24, 26, and *Journal of Royal Asiatic Society of Bengal* 5, no. 1 (n.d.): 168, in *Sources of Indian Tradition*, vol. 1, *From the Beginning to 1800*, ed. Ainslie T. Embree (New York: Columbia University Press, 1988), 472–73.

39

Na't, *Devotional Poetry*

Na't *is a type of devotional poetry written in Urdu that was performed in South Asia at least as early as the seventeenth century. It consists of recitations in praise of the Prophet, members of his family (the* Ahl-i Bayt*), and other esteemed Muslims, such as the thirteenth-century Sufi Mu'inuddin Chishti (popularly known as Khwaja Gharib Nawaz).* Na't *poetry, performed largely by Sunni Muslims, recalls Shi'a traditions, specifically, the tragic events of the Battle of Karbala, in which the Prophet's grandson Husayn (or Husain) and his followers were killed. The Prophet, who is sometimes presented as a monarch presiding over his court assembly (*darbar*), is almost always the central figure in these poems. Their recitation reinforced for both speaker and listeners the notion of Muhammad's ongoing spiritual presence in their lives.*

Na't *of the Prophet*

ca. 1600

Every believer is intoxicated with the one whose name is Muhammad
Love for him elevates one in this world and the hereafter
The prophet's mercy pervades both worlds, every divine blessing is
    due to him
He who has affection in his heart for him, also pleases the Supreme
    Lord
He belongs to Allah
Every believer is intoxicated with the one whose name is Muhammad
Love for him elevates one in this world and the hereafter
He is the basis of everything else; he is the guide on the path of Allah
He is the chief of all prophets and ranks right after Allah
He is the first among all creatures

Patrick Eisenlohr, "*Na't*: Media Contexts and Transnational Dimensions of a Devotional Practice," in *Islam in South Asia in Practice*, ed. Barbara D. Metcalf (Princeton, N.J.: Princeton University Press, 2009), 109–10.

Every believer is intoxicated with the one whose name is Muhammad
Love for him elevates one in this world and the hereafter
He cut the moon in half and the set sun rose again
If he wishes, seventy persons can be fed with a single cup of milk
Every believer is intoxicated with the one whose name is Muhammad
Love for him elevates one in this world and the hereafter
In all difficulties of life, at the moment of death, or in the tomb
He will protect us wherever we are, and also on the Day of Judgment
His grace supports us
Every believer is intoxicated with the one whose name is Muhammad
Love for him elevates one in this world and the hereafter
I ruined my whole life in sinful deeds,
The only hope I have is his benevolent glance
Allah willing, Bilal Anwar will also receive the grace of his splendid
    appearance, which will illuminate his tomb
Every believer is intoxicated with the one whose name is Muhammad
Love for him elevates one in this world and the hereafter

In the Garden of the Prophet

ca. 1600

In the garden of the Prophet, you are the most beautiful flower
O Husayn, my salutations to You
The one who is a martyr for divine truth never dies
These are not my words, but those of the Supreme Lord himself
In the garden of the Prophet, you are the most beautiful flower
O Husayn, my salutations to You
My friends, how beautiful is his last prayer
Prostrating himself before his creator even under the enemy's
    blade, this is my imam
In the garden of the Prophet, you are the most beautiful flower
O Husayn, my salutations to you
Every human being hates the accursed Yazid

Patrick Eisenlohr, "*Na't*: Media Contexts and Transnational Dimensions of a Devotional Practice," in *Islam in South Asia in Practice*, ed. Barbara D. Metcalf (Princeton, N.J.: Princeton University Press, 2009), 110.

For every heart is a servant of the child of the Lion of Allah[1]
In the garden of the Prophet, you are the most beautiful flower
O Husayn, my salutations to You
For the sake of the progeny of Muhammad
O Ehsan, may their murderers be strictly banned from paradise
In the garden of the Prophet, you are the most beautiful flower
O Husayn, my salutations to You

[1] Ali, Husayn's father and the Prophet's son-in law.

40

ABD UL-HAQQ AL-DIHLAWI AL-BUKHARI

The Perfection of Faith

ca. 1650

The excerpts in this document exemplify the use of reason and tradition to justify orthodox beliefs in premodern Indian Islam. They are taken from the seventeenth-century Sunni doctrine called The Perfection of Faith, *written by Abd ul-Haqq al-Dihlawi al-Bukhari. Abd ul-Haqq was one of the most famous Sunni writers in Mughal India. After performing the Hajj and studying in the Hijaz, he taught in Delhi for nearly five decades. Abd ul-Haqq wrote biographies of the Prophet Muhammad and Indian Muslim saints (pirs), commentaries on the traditions of the Prophet, and a history of India. His main contribution to Islam in India was helping to popularize the study of the Hadith.*

The Attributes of Allah

The attributes of Allah are eternal and are of equal duration with His essence. Whatever He possesses—perfection and reality—is constant in eternity; because the location of accidents was created, it does not become

---

Abd ul-Haqq al-Dihlawī al-Bukhārī, *Takmīl ul-Imān*, fols. 2a–3b, 13–15, in *Sources of Indian Tradition*, vol. 1, *From the Beginning to 1800*, ed. Ainslie T. Embree (New York: Columbia University Press, 1988), 393–97.

eternal. Except in a body there is neither limitation, cause, nor time; the creator of the world is not body and substance. . . . He is not a body and an attribute, that is to say, with the bodily qualities which the body has, like blackness and whiteness. He is not formed so that He has bodily shape and He is not compounded so that He is joined together repeatedly. He is not numbered so that it is possible to count Him. He is not limited so that He has a limit and He is not in a direction, that is to say, He is not above or below, before or after, left or right. He is not in a place and not in a moment, because all these are attributes of the world and the Nourisher of the World is not subject to worldly attributes and His purposes are not subject to time. Time does not include or circumscribe Him. His existence is not dependent upon time. For in that condition when there was not time, there was He. Now also there is time and He exists. Therefore, He is not in time.

Free Will

First it is necessary to understand the meaning of compulsion and choice so that the essence of this problem may become clear. Man's actions are of two kinds. One, when he conceives something, and, if that thing is desired by and is agreeable to his nature, a great desire and passion for it wells up from within him, and he follows that passion and moves after it. Or if the thing is contrary and repugnant to him, dislike and abhorrence for it wells up within him and he shuns it. His relation to the action and to stopping the action before the appearance of the desire and the loathing were on a par. It was possible that he might act or not act, whether at the stage of conception when the power to act was near, or before conceiving the idea when he was farther from acting. This motion of man is called an optional motion and the action which results from that motion is called an optional action. The other kind of action is when there is no conception, arousing of desire and wish, but motion occurs and then desire, like the trembling of a leaf. This motion is called compulsory and obligatory. If the meaning of desire and intention (as distinct from choice) is as stated, it may be objected: "Who says that man is not discerning and is not perspicacious? The creation of man occurred by choice, and such is the composition of his nature. Who says that all human motions and actions are compulsory? To say this is to deny virtue. No intelligent person will agree to this."

But there are difficulties in this conclusion. For, if, after comprehension and conversance with the eternal knowledge, intentions, decree, and ordination of Allah, it is conceived that it is not (really) man who brings actions into existence, that conclusion will be reached because it is realized that if Allah knew from all eternity that a particular action must be performed by a particular individual, that action must therefore be so performed, whether without that individual's choice, as in compulsory motion, or with his choice. If the action was optional (in form), the individual did not (really) have choice either in his decision or in his action. Furthermore, although the individual may have had choice in his action, yet he did not have any choice in its first beginnings.

For example, when an eye opens and does not see, there is no image before it. If after seeing and observing visible objects, they are desired, a rousing of passion and desire is compulsory and the existence of motion toward them is also obligatory. Thereafter, although this action occurs through the human being's choice, yet in fact this choice is obligatory and compulsory upon him. Obligation and necessity are contrary to the reality of choice. Man has choice but he has not choice in his choice; or to put it another way, he has choice in appearance, but in fact he is acting under compulsion. . . . Imam Ja'far Sadiq, who is a master of the people of the Sufi way and a chief of the people of Truth, says that there is no compulsion or freedom. But he lays down that the truth is to be found between compulsion and freedom. The Jabarites are those who say that fundamentally man has no choice and his motions are like those of inanimate nature. The Qadiriyyah are those who say that man has a choice and that man is independent in his transactions. His actions are his own creations. Imam Ja'far says that both these two schools of thought are false and go to extremes. The true school of thought is to be found between them but reason is at a loss and confounded in the comprehension of this middle way; in truth this confusion is found among people of a disputatious and contending sort who wish to found articles of faith upon reason, and who will not acknowledge anything as true and believe in it unless it pleases their reason and falls within their understanding. But for believers, the short proof of this is what is put forward in the Holy Law and the Qur'an, in which it is written on this problem that Allah has both power and will and, notwithstanding that, He charges obedience and disobedience to His servants. And He says, Allah never commits injustice but men have inflicted injustice upon themselves. "Allah was not one to wrong them but they did wrong themselves."

41

IBN 'UMAR MIHRABI

The Indian Proof

ca. 1615

*The Indian Proof, written during the early seventeenth century by Ibn
'Umar Mihrabi, attempts to counter Hindu religious influences among
Muslims living in rural villages away from urban Islamic culture. It is
in the form of a fictional dialogue between a* sharak *(a mythical talking
bird), which asks questions on cosmology and religion, and a parrot,
which provides the proper Muslim responses.*

The sharak said: Please be kind enough to explain the manner of the coming into being of all creation and of everything which exists—mankind,
the angels, jinns [supernatural creatures in Islamic mythology], devils,
animals like wild beasts, birds, vegetation like trees and plants, the soul
and the lower self of man and animals, the earth, mountains, seas, dry
land and water, fire, wind, the skies, the world and the constellations, the
signs of the zodiac, the mansions and the empyrean [celestial], the throne
of Allah, the tablet, the pen, heaven, hell, the dwelling place in time and
space of all these. Through your generous instruction it should become
clear and known to everyone without doubt or obscurity what is the reality of each, in a way which explains its creation and reassures the heart
and mind. And also, when you explain, do it so that all doubts disappear,
reality is distinguishable from error and truth from falsehood.

The parrot answered: Know that the Way of Eternity (Marsad ul-Abad)
gives an explanation of the beginning of created existences in this world
and in heaven which has become the mode of existent things. If Allah
wills, this explanation will be repeated. Now listen with your mind and
from your heart to this other explanation. There is a difference between
human souls and the pure soul of Muhammad the Prophet. As the
prophets have said, he was the first thing Allah created. They called him

Muhammad Mujir Wajib Adib, *Miftāh al-Jinan*, fols. 4b, 9b–10, 13b, 14b, 20b–21a; Abd
ul-Haqq al-Dihlawī al-Bukhārī, *Takmīl ul-Īmān*, fols. 2a–3b, 13–15; Ibn 'Umar Mihrābi,
Hujjat ul-Hind, fols. 11b–13a, in Theodore de Bary, *Sources of Indian Tradition* (New
York: Columbia University Press, 1958), 398–99.

a light and a spirit and he himself was the existence of existences, the fruit and the tree of created beings. As the tradition said, "But for you the heavens would not have been created"; for this, and no other, was the way in which creation began, like as a tree from whose seed spring the chief fruits of the tree. Then Allah Most High, when He wished to create created beings, first brought forth the light of Muhammad's soul from the ray of the light of His Unity as is reported in the Prophetic traditions. "I am from Allah and the believers are from me." In some traditions it is reported that Allah looked with a loving eye upon that light of Muhammad. Modesty overcame Him and the tears dropped from Him. From those drops He created the souls of the prophets. From those lights He created the souls of the saints, from their souls, the souls of believers, and from the souls of the believers He created the souls of the disobedient. From the souls of the disobedient He created the souls of hypocrites and infidels. From human souls He created the souls of the angels and from the rays of the souls of the angels He created the souls of jinns, and from their souls, devils. He created the different souls of animals according to their different kinds of ranks and states, all their descriptions of beings and souls—vegetation and minerals and compounds and elements He also brought forth.

To explain the remainder of creation; from the pearl [teardrop] which had remained, Allah created a jewel and looked upon that jewel with a majestic glance. With that awesome glance Allah melted that jewel and it became half water and half fire. Then He caused warm smoke to rise from the fire and the water and to be suspended in the air. From that came the seven heavens and from the sparks which were in the air with the smoke came forth the twinkling constellations. When He had brought forth the sun and the moon, the stars, the signs of the zodiac and the mansions of the moon from the leaping tongues of flame, He threw the wind and the water into confusion; foam appeared upon the surface and forth came the seven surfaces of the earth. Waves rose up and mountains emerged therefrom. From the remainder of the water Allah created the seas. He created the world in six days.

A Chronology of Islam in the Indian Ocean World (570–1704)

570	Prophet Muhammad born in Mecca.
614	A group of Muslims first migrate from Mecca to the Christian kingdom of Aksum, Ethiopia.
618–907	Tang dynasty in China.
622	Hijra, the flight of Muslims from Mecca to Medina; Year One of the Muslim calendar (1 AH).
632	Prophet Muhammad dies in Medina.
661–750	Umayyad caliphate establishes the first Islamic empire, based in Damascus.
712–715	Conquest of Sind by Arabs under Muhammad Ibn Qasim.
750–1258	Abbasid caliphate rules from Baghdad.
786–809	Abbasid caliphate of Harun al-Rashid marks a flowering of Islamic culture and science.
869–883	Zanj rebellion against the Abbasid regime in southern Iraq.
900	Coastal strip from Zeila to the tip of the Horn of Africa Islamized.
960–1279	Song dynasty in China.
969–1171	Fatimid caliphate in Egypt.
1055	Seljuk Turks capture Baghdad and establish rule over Mesopotamia.

1100   Islam extends down the East African coast to Zanzibar and
           Mozambique.

1169–
1250   Ayyubids defeat Fatimids and rule Egypt.

ca.
1190   Muslim Indians begin to establish themselves in Southeast Asia.

1211–
1526   Delhi sultanate in northern India, beginning with reign of Iltutmish.

1250–
1517   Mamluks, originally slave-soldiers, rule Egypt.

1258   Mongols, nomadic tribes from Asia, sack Baghdad, ending the
           Abbasid caliphate.

1271–
1295   Travels of the Venetian merchant Marco Polo to China.

1271–
1368   Mongols rule China as Yuan dynasty.

1295–
1304   Reign of Ghazan as Ilkhan; conversion of Ilkhan Mongols to Islam.

1324   Mali emperor Mansa Musa reaches Mecca on Hajj, passes
           through Cairo.

1325–
1354   Moroccan qadi Ibn Battuta travels across Muslim Africa and Asia.

1336–
1565   Hindu-ruled Vijayanagar kingdom in southern India.

1368–
1644   Ming dynasty in China.

1382   North African scholar Ibn Khaldun becomes professor of Islamic
           law at Cairo.

1400–
1450   Great Zimbabwe, in southeastern Africa, reaches peak of
           prosperity.

1405–
1433   Chinese Muslim admiral Zheng He's expeditions in Southeast
           Asia and across the Indian Ocean.

1415   Adal sultanate established in the Horn of Africa.

1453   Ottoman conquest of Constantinople marks fall of the Byzantine
           Empire.

1469   Guru Nanak, founder of Sikhism, born.

1498 Portuguese Vasco da Gama circumnavigates Africa and enters the Indian Ocean.

1501 Safavid dynasty in Persia imposes Shi'ism as the state religion.

1510 Portuguese take control of Goa, India.

1511 Portuguese take control of Malacca.

1526 Battle of Panipat; Mughal Babur displaces Lodis as rulers of Delhi and Agra.

1530 Consolidation of Aceh under Sultan Ali Mughayat Shah.

1556–
1605 Reign of Mughal emperor Akbar.

1571 Ottoman fleet defeated at Lepanto, in the eastern Mediterranean.

1600 English East India Company founded.

1602 Dutch East India Company founded.

1605–
1627 Reign of Mughal emperor Jahangir.

1607–
1626 Malik Ambar regent minister of Ahmednagar sultanate.

1641 Dutch take control of Malacca.

1641–
1699 Rule of female sultans in Aceh, beginning with Sultana Taj al-Alam Safiyat al-Din Shah.

1657–
1658 War of succession between Dara Shikoh and Aurangzeb in Mughal Empire.

1704 Antoine Galland publishes first European translation of *The Thousand and One Nights*.

Questions for Consideration

1. What economic, political, and environmental factors facilitated trade, migration, and the spread of Islam across the Indian Ocean world?

2. Compare and contrast the ways in which Islam entered into societies in East Africa, South Asia, and Southeast Asia, providing evidence from the documents in your answer.

3. Describe the relationship between seafaring peoples and the agricultural empires in the interior of the Indian Ocean world.

4. Which religions and spiritual practices competed with Islam in this vast region, and how successful were they in resisting or adopting Islam?

5. What evidence from the documents suggests the cultural and political impact of the spread of Islam?

6. How was Islam Afro-Asianized? How were East Africa and South and Southeast Asia Islamized?

7. Which political powers in the Indian Ocean world demanded religious conformity, and which were tolerant of various religions?

8. How was language used in the spread and adoption of Islam?

9. How did the rise of Islam and the establishment of Muslim sultanates and empires affect existing trade relations?

10. Discuss the different kinds of documents that can be used to re-create the history of Islam in this region. What do such documents reveal, and what do they conceal?

11. What impact did the spread of Islam have on the legal systems of the people who adopted it?

12. What impact did Muslim law (Shari'a) have on those who did not adopt the religion?

13. To what extent did gender relations change with the advent of Islam? What did those changes entail?

14. What role did Muslims play in the slave trade across the Indian Ocean world?

15. How did Sufis help spread Islam in South and Southeast Asia?
16. In what ways did local customs change with the coming of Islam? In what ways did they not change? Provide some examples.
17. To what extent did Islam create a sense of common identity among its adherents?

Selected Bibliography

Adas, Michael. *Islamic and European Expansion: The Forging of a Global Order*. Philadelphia: Temple University Press, 1993.

Ahmed, Leila. *Women and Gender in Islam: Historical Roots of a Modern Debate*. New Haven, Conn.: Yale University Press, 1992.

al-Musawi, Muhsin. Introduction and notes to *The Arabian Nights*. New York: Barnes & Noble Classics, 2007.

Alpers, Edward. *The Indian Ocean in World History*. New York: Oxford University Press, 2014.

Aslan, Reza. *No God, but God: The Origins, Evolution, and Future of Islam*. New York: Random House, 2005.

Azra, Azyumardi. *Islam in the Indonesian World: An Account of Institutional Formation*. Bandung: Mizan Pustaka, 2006.

Casale, Giancarlo. *The Ottoman Age of Exploration*. New York: Oxford University Press, 2010.

Chaudhuri, K. N. *Trade and Civilisation in the Indian Ocean: An Economic History from the Rise of Islam to 1750*. Cambridge: Cambridge University Press, 2002.

Dunn, Ross E. *The Adventures of Ibn Battuta: A Muslim Traveler of the Fourteenth Century*. Berkeley: University of California Press, 2005.

Eaton, Richard. *India's Islamic Traditions, 711–1750*. New Delhi: Oxford University Press, 2004.

Embree, Ainslie T., ed. *Sources of Indian Tradition*. Vol. 1, *From the Beginning to 1800*. New York: Columbia University Press, 1988.

Freeman-Grenville, G. S. P. *The East African Coast: Select Documents from the First to the Earlier Nineteenth Century*. Oxford: Clarendon Press, 1962.

Hall, Kenneth R. *A History of Early Southeast Asia: Maritime Trade and Societal Development, 100–1500*. Lanham, Md.: Rowman & Littlefield, 2011.

Hodgson, Marshall G. S. *The Venture of Islam*. Vol. 2, *The Expansion of Islam in the Middle Periods*. Chicago: University of Chicago Press, 1961.

Jayasuriya, Shihan de Silva, and Richard Pankhurst, eds. *The African Diaspora in the Indian Ocean*. Trenton, N.J.: Africa World Press, 2003.

Levathes, Louise. *When China Ruled the Seas: The Treasure Fleet of the Dragon Throne, 1405–1433*. New York: Oxford University Press, 1994.

Levtzion, Nehemia, and Randall L. Pouwels, eds. *The History of Islam in Africa*. Athens: Ohio University Press, 2000.

Lewis, Bernard. *Race and Slavery in the Middle East: An Historical Enquiry*. New York: Oxford University Press, 1990.

Lipman, Jonathan N. *Familiar Strangers: A History of Muslims in Northwest China*. Seattle: University of Washington Press, 1997.

Loimeier, Roman. *Muslim Societies in Africa: A Historical Anthropology*. Bloomington: Indiana University Press, 2014.

Margariti, Roxani Eleni. *Aden and the Indian Ocean Trade: 150 Years in the Life of a Medieval Arabian Port*. Chapel Hill: University of North Carolina Press, 2007.

Metcalf, Barbara D., ed. *Islam in South Asia in Practice*. Princeton, N.J.: Princeton University Press, 2009.

Nurse, Derek, and Thomas Spear. *The Swahili: Reconstructing the History and Language of an African Society, 800–1500*. Philadelphia: University of Pennsylvania Press, 1985.

Parker, John, and Richard Rathbone. *African History: A Very Short Introduction*. New York: Oxford University Press, 2003.

Pearson, Michael. *The Indian Ocean*. New York: Routledge, 2003.

Pipes, Daniel. *Slave Soldiers and Islam: The Genesis of a Military System*. New Haven, Conn.: Yale University Press, 1981.

Pires, Tomé. *Suma Oriental of Tomé Pires: An Account of the East, from the Red Sea to China, Written in Malacca and India in 1512–1515*, ed. Armando Cortesão. London: Hakluyt Society, 1944.

Reid, Anthony, ed. *Southeast Asia in the Early Modern Era: Trade, Power, and Belief*. Ithaca, N.Y.: Cornell University Press, 1993.

Ricci, Ronit. *Islam Translated: Literature, Conversion, and the Arabic Cosmopolis of South and Southeast Asia*. Chicago: University of Chicago Press, 2011.

Risso, Patricia. *Merchants and Faith: Muslim Commerce and Culture in the Indian Ocean*. Boulder, Colo.: Westview Press, 1995.

Robinson, David. *Muslim Societies in African History*. Cambridge: Cambridge University Press. 2004.

Sheriff, Abdul. *Dhow Cultures of the Indian Ocean: Cosmopolitanism, Commerce, and Islam*. New York: Columbia University Press, 2010.

Trimingham, J. Spencer. *The Sufi Orders in Islam*. New York: Oxford University Press, 1998.

WEB-BASED RESOURCES

Ali, Omar H. "The African Diaspora in the Indian Ocean World" (essays and exhibition). Schomburg Center for Research in Black Culture, New York Public Library, 2011. http://exhibitions.nypl.org/africansindianocean/index2.php.

Annenberg Learner. *The Indian Ocean World* (video). Bridging World History, Unit 10: Connections across Water. http://www.learner.org/courses/worldhistory/unit_video_10-1.html?pop=yes&pid=2153.

Center for South Asian and Indian Ocean Studies, Tufts University, Medford, Mass. http://as.tufts.edu/csaios/.

Halsall, Paul. *Internet Islamic History Sourcebook*. Fordham University, New York. http://www.fordham.edu/halsall/islam/islamsbook.asp.

"The Indian Ocean and Global Trade." Special Issue, *Saudi Aramco World*, July/August 2005. http://www.aramcoworld.com/issue/200504/default.htm.

The Indian Ocean in World History (Web site). Sultan Qaboos Cultural Center, Washington, D.C. http://www.indianoceanhistory.org.

Indian Ocean World Centre, McGill University, Montreal. http://indianoceanworldcentre.com/.

"Materiality of Indian Ocean Connections." British Museum, London. http://www.britishmuseum.org/research/research_projects/all_current_projects/indian_ocean_connections.aspx.

Sealinks Project, University of Oxford. http://www.sealinksproject.com/.

"Sultans of Deccan India, 1500–1700: Opulence and Fantasy" (exhibition). Metropolitan Museum of Art, New York. http://www.metmuseum.org/exhibitions/listings/2015/deccan-sultans.

Acknowledgments (continued from p. iv)

Document 1: Ibn Battuta, *The Travels of Ibn Battuta*, translated by H. A. R. Gibb. Hakluyt Society, 1958–1994. Used by permission of the Hakluyt Society.

Document 3: Ma Huan, *Ying-Yai Sheng-lan, The Overall Survey of the Ocean's Shores* (1433), translated by Feng Ch'eng-Chun, J. V. G. Mills. Cambridge: Cambridge University Press, 1970. Used by permission of the Hakluyt Society.

Document 6: [Part 1] G. R. Tibbetts, *Arab Navigation in the Indian Ocean before the Portuguese*. London: The Royal Asiatic Society of Great Britain and Ireland, 1971. Used by permission.

Documents 7, 26, 28 (parts I and II), 31 (parts I and II), 32, 39 (parts I and II): *Islam in South Asia in Practice*, by Barbara Daly Metcalf. Reproduced with permission of Princeton University Press in the format Book via Copyright Clearance Center.

Document 8: Tomé Pires, *Suma Oriental of Tomé Pires: An Account of the East, from the Red Sea to China. Written in Malacca and India in 1512–1515*, edited by Armando Cortesão. Hakluyt Society, 1944. Used by permission of the Hakluyt Society.

Document 15: [Part 1] From: John Hunwick and Eve Troutt Powell, *The African Diaspora in the Mediterranean Lands of Islam*, pp. 8–9. © Markus Wiener Publishers 2002. Used by permission of the publisher.

Document 15: [Part 2] *Race and Slavery in the Middle East: An Historical Enquiry* by Bernard Lewis (1992), 324w, from "The Rights of the Slave," pp. 146–47. © 1992 by Oxford University Press, Inc. By permission of Oxford University Press, USA.

Document 16: *Corpus of Early African Sources for West African History*, edited by Nehemiah Levtzion and translated by John F. P. Hopkins. Copyright © 1981 University of Ghana, International Academic Union and Cambridge University Press. Reprinted with permission of Cambridge University Press.

Document 17: *Race and Slavery in the Middle East: An Historical Enquiry* by Bernard Lewis (1992), 488w, from p. 148. © 1992 by Oxford University Press, Inc. By permission of Oxford University Press, USA.

Document 18: Based on translation by Abdullah Yusuf Ali, *The Holy Qur'ān*. Elmhurst, N.Y.: Tahrike Tarsile Qur'ān, 1987. Used by permission.

Document 19: Sahih Al-Bukhari, *The Translation of the Meanings of (the Hadith)*, translated by Muhammad Muhsin Khan, compiled by Al-Imam Zain-ud-Din Ahmad bin Abdul-Lateef Az-Zubaidi. Riyadh, Saudi Arabia: Dar-us-Salam Publications. Used by permission of Dar-us-Salam Publications.

Document 27: [Part 1] *The Travels of Ibn Jubayr* by R. J. C. Broadhurst. Published by Pimlico. Reprinted by permission of The Random House Group Limited.

Documents 30, 36, 37, 38 (parts I and II), 40: From *Sources of Indian Tradition, Volume 1: From the Beginning to 1800*, edited by Ainslie T. Embree. Copyright © 1988 Columbia University Press. Reprinted by permission of the publisher.

Document 35: Kulliyāt-i ghazalīyāt-i Khusraw [*The Complete Ghazals of Khusraw*], ed. Iqbāl Salāh al-Dīn and Sayyid Vazīr al-Hasan 'Ābidī, 4 vols. Lahore, 1972–1974, vol. 1, pp. 362–63, ghazal 190. Translated by Alyssa Gabbay.

Document 41: From *Sources of Indian Tradition*, by Theodore de Bary. Copyright © 1958 Columbia University Press. Reprinted by permission of the publisher.

Index